Elements in New Religious Movements
Series Editor
Rebecca Moore
San Diego State University
Founding Editor
†James R. Lewis
Wuhan University

WEARING THEIR FAITH

New Religious Movements, Dress, and Fashion in America

Lynn S. Neal
Wake Forest University

Shaftesbury Road, Cambridge CB2 8EA, United Kingdom

One Liberty Plaza, 20th Floor, New York, NY 10006, USA

477 Williamstown Road, Port Melbourne, VIC 3207, Australia

314–321, 3rd Floor, Plot 3, Splendor Forum, Jasola District Centre, New Delhi – 110025, India

103 Penang Road, #05–06/07, Visioncrest Commercial, Singapore 238467

Cambridge University Press is part of Cambridge University Press & Assessment, a department of the University of Cambridge.

We share the University's mission to contribute to society through the pursuit of education, learning and research at the highest international levels of excellence.

www.cambridge.org
Information on this title: www.cambridge.org/9781009619059

DOI: 10.1017/9781009304641

© Lynn S. Neal 2025

This publication is in copyright. Subject to statutory exception and to the provisions of relevant collective licensing agreements, no reproduction of any part may take place without the written permission of Cambridge University Press & Assessment.

When citing this work, please include a reference to the DOI 10.1017/9781009304641

First published 2025

A catalogue record for this publication is available from the British Library

ISBN 978-1-009-61905-9 Hardback
ISBN 978-1-009-30465-8 Paperback
ISSN 2635-232X (online)
ISSN 2635-2311 (print)

Cambridge University Press & Assessment has no responsibility for the persistence or accuracy of URLs for external or third-party internet websites referred to in this publication and does not guarantee that any content on such websites is, or will remain, accurate or appropriate.

Wearing Their Faith

New Religious Movements, Dress, and Fashion in America

Elements in New Religious Movements

DOI: 10.1017/9781009304641
First published online: January 2025

Lynn S. Neal
Wake Forest University
Author for correspondence: Lynn S. Neal, nealls@wfu.edu

Abstract: New religious movements (NRMs) have a long, interconnected history with distinct forms of dress and clothing. However, research on NRMs has not focused sufficiently on the clothing and material culture of these groups. In response, this Element examines the central role that dress plays in the creation of charismatic leaders and the formation of faithful followers. Through a variety of case studies – ranging from Maharishi Mahesh Yogi to Father Divine, from the Children of God to the Nation of Islam – we see how dress and fashion practices provide people with a powerful way to live and wear their faith. In addition, the fashion industry takes note and incorporates ideas about cults and clothing into their trends and styles. In doing so, it fuels the cult stereotype and fosters normative understandings of what constitutes good religion.

Keywords: clothing, dress, fashion, new religious movements, cults

© Lynn S. Neal 2025

ISBNs: 9781009619059 (HB), 9781009304658 (PB), 9781009304641 (OC)
ISSNs: 2635-232X (online), 2635-2311 (print)

Contents

	Introduction	1
1	Clothing and the Creation of the Cult Leader	4
2	Dress and the Devotion of NRM Followers	27
3	Fashion and the Maintenance of the Cult Stereotype	47
4	Concluding Thoughts	69
	References	71

Introduction

On any given day in the United States and around the globe, people put on jewelry featuring a cross or crucifix – necklaces, bracelets, and brooches. For some it is a marker of religious identity, for others a beloved gift from their grandmother, for some a fashion statement, and for still others it is all or some combination of these things. Silver or gold, wooden or glass, cross jewelry is ubiquitous, a visible and unremarked-upon symbol of faith and fashion. Even though they are encountered less often, people accept and even admire the simplicity of dress and lifestyle embodied by Amish and Mennonite communities, and while those seen wearing Christian T-shirts might not be at the leading edge of fashion, they are viewed as devout. Yet, when those from groups labeled cults wear clothing and jewelry representative of their respective traditions, they are deemed as having an unhealthy and excessive devotion to their religion, which is fueled by the cult stereotype.

Since the 1950s, the media and many people conceptualize new religious movements (NRMs) as cults, a label that comes with a host of biased and superficial ideas. The cult stereotype usually includes a charismatic leader (deluded by his own deviant beliefs or using those beliefs to con others) who has duped and exploited vulnerable followers through deceptive recruitment practices. These manipulated followers are then led down a path of religious excess, financial misdeeds, and sexual exploitation, while being isolated from their concerned families and the practices that constitute so-called religion and normal life. Scholars Jane Dillon and James Richardson (1994) characterize the stereotype as hegemonic, given its wide usage and acceptance. They argue that applying the cult label to these religious groups prevents people from questioning the concept, its application, and its repercussions, which continues to foster these views.

The popular media plays a vital role in the creation and maintenance of the hegemonic cult stereotype. TV shows of all genres have utilized it to enliven their storylines, attract viewers, and uphold dominant views of what constitutes legitimate religion (Neal 2011). From *Mork and Mindy* to *The Unbreakable Kimmy Schmidt*, from *Knight Rider* to *Law and Order*, this negative framing endures. The advent of streaming services has only amplified and emboldened this trend. Recent shows featuring fictional or historical cults, including *The Path* (Hulu 2016–2018), *Sacred Lies* (Facebook Watch 2018), and *The Leftovers* (HBO 2014–2017), as well as *Waco* (Paramount 2018) and *Wild Wild Country* (Netflix 2018), speak to the enduring allure of the evil cult trope in American society.

Media scholar Marita Sturken describes the power of visual media. "For much of the American public, docudramas are a primary source of historical information. They afford a means through which uncomfortable histories of traumatic events can be smoothed over, retold, and ascribed new meanings" (1997: 85). These forms of entertainment media provide viewers with reassuring storylines in which deceptive recruiting practices are exposed, fraudulent cult leaders are brought to justice, and victimized cult members are freed. Moreover, they offer viewers a vision of the past as they rework, retell, and re-envision controversial cult-related events, including the events at Jonestown (1978), the standoff with the Branch Davidians outside of Waco, Texas (1993), and the Heaven's Gate suicides in San Diego, California (1997) (Neal 2014a).

Taken all together these various media forms reinforce the cult stereotype and create a powerful set of visual culture norms that define what NRMs look like, including where they live and what they do. These shows commonly depict cult members living in isolated and rural areas (wilderness) in contrast to the city (civilization). Communal living, rather than nuclear family life, functions as another visual element that differentiates the cults from the presumed norm. Showing unfamiliar and seemingly dangerous rituals further separates deluded cult practice from enlightened religious or secular belief. Further, the charismatic leader and the typical cult devotee embody this deviance, which can be seen not only in their beliefs and practices but also in how they dress (Neal 2011: 89–93).

Clothing represents a significant element that displays the peculiarity of cults to viewers. There is an expectation that so-called cult members dress differently – that sartorial strangeness identifies and marks their religious deviance. Typically, TV shows represent this through the donning of seemingly odd and/or uniform clothing that symbolizes the unusual and unhealthy level of devotion deceived converts extend to a fraudulent leader. For example, when the Simpson family joins the Movementarians they begin wearing long flowing robes, while Robert from *Everybody Loves Raymond* dons a festive Hawaiian shirt, and *The Unbreakable Kimmy Schmidt* emerges from an underground bunker in a long, pastel blue prairie dress (Neal 2011: 88).

Visually representing cult clothing as homogenous and distinct from the mainstream reinforces the cult stereotype. It emphasizes the contrast between American norms in which clothing symbolizes individual choice and freedom of expression and cult deviance where clothing represents loss of personal autonomy, communal commitment, and extreme religious devotion. Clothing, then, becomes a shortcut to express the danger of cults as it represents the erasure of individuality and freedom that observers associate with these groups. It also functions to reassure audiences that such religious deviance can be easily seen, recognized, and presumably addressed implicitly or explicitly through some form of social control.

The repeated portrayal of cult clothing as distinct and identifiable has become a constituent part of American cultural memory. However, given the pervasiveness of these depictions and the ways cultural memory weaves together history and desire, we know little beyond these superficial characterizations. Some scholars have helpfully attended to the role of clothing within the context of a specific group. For example, Colleen McDannell (1995) examined the significance of Mormon undergarments and Elizabeth Bucar (2017) has analyzed the intersection of Islam, dress, and fashion. Yet, few scholarly studies have focused on the broader function of clothing within NRMs. *Wearing Their Faith* addresses this oversight and answers a variety of questions. What is the role of clothing in NRMs? How does clothing help create and foster the idea of charismatic leadership? Why would a religious group choose to dress differently? What is the relationship between clothing choices and religious identity? How do NRMs use clothing to challenge broader cultural norms and ideas? And how are ideas about cult clothing shaped by and reflected in the fashion industry?

Wearing Their Faith analyzes the vital role that clothing plays in the formation of NRM leaders and followers. Through careful research and illustrative case studies it challenges the superficial understanding of the cult/clothing relationship promoted by the cult stereotype. This examination demonstrates the significance of clothing in religious life. Rather than being a trivial component or accessory, clothing and clothing choices help mediate and constitute religion, new or old. Scholar David Morgan argues: "By shifting attention to what people do, and understanding belief as grounded in practice, we open the door for substantive analysis of the materiality of religion since making, exchanging, displaying, and using artifacts are principal aspects of human doing." By doing so, we can better understand "the embodied, material features of lived religion" of various groups, including NRMs (2010: 6–7).

Wearing Their Faith examines these questions through three thematic sections. Section 1 focuses on the role of clothing in relation to one individual – the charismatic cult leader. In the eyes of the public, these leaders are often the primary focus of media attention and come to represent the group. Internally, charismatic leaders are believed to wield tremendous power and influence given their inspired status. Thus, how they are represented and what they wear carries great significance. This section examines how charismatic leaders dress and why. It also analyzes the connections between dress and religious authority. Section 2 shifts the lens to how clothing functions for followers in NRMs. By examining case studies, it analyzes why followers dress in particular ways in light of a movement's theology and historical context. It also examines how NRMs use their clothing choices to navigate existing perceptions and American norms. Distinct clothing not only sets NRM members apart from the dominant society, but it also implicitly or explicitly challenges dimensions of that society. Section 3 directs our attention to the intersection of so-called cults and the fashion industry. It looks closely at 2018 and the emergence of what some refer to as cultcore in fashion magazines and on the runway. It asks: What types of clothing were classified as cultlike? What NRMs inspired these trends and why? How do these conceptions reinforce (or challenge) stereotypical views? As we explore these questions, we'll examine how the fashion industry constructs some NRMs as more fashionable than others, but, ultimately, these groups continue to be constrained by the dominant cult paradigm. A brief final section presents some concluding reflections.

Before we begin this journey into sartorial choices, a brief discussion of terminology is important. First, in the study of new religions, scholars continue to debate nomenclature. While the cult label has been widely criticized by scholars, as documented earlier, it continues to hold the most salience with the general public. "New religious movement" has become one prominent, but not unproblematic, preference as it raises questions about newness and continued debates about the category of religion. These debates are important, and demand continued attention; however, they are not the focus of this Element. Thus, I use the word "cult" at times to draw attention to the stereotype and dominant discourses surrounding these groups. I also use the label NRM throughout.

1 Clothing and the Creation of the Cult Leader

On October 13, 1975, the cover of *Time* magazine featured a painting of the Maharishi Mahesh Yogi. On a dark blue and black background, the close-up rendering of the Maharishi highlights his upward gaze and his distinct appearance. His long hair and beard are a glowing white in contrast to his brown skin, orange robes, and the colorful flowers surrounding him. Given the smile on his face, he appears happy, and his upward gaze suggests spiritual inspiration; however, the dominating headline, "Meditation: The Answer to All Your Problems?," combined with the dark background, creates a sense of doubt and suspicion. The cover image, like other media representations and articles, focuses on the NRM leader as the key to unlocking the mysteries and mayhem associated with cults.

In many ways the hegemonic cult stereotype revolves around the persona of the villainous cult leader. These often-male figures are associated with several negative traits that become essentialized and fixed in the stereotype (Hall 1997: 257). These traits include, but are not limited to, authoritarianism, exploitativeness, deceitfulness, dishonesty, sexual depravity, violence, and delusion. The stereotype emphasizes how the leader misuses his power to victimize others for his own aggrandizement and benefit. Given these asymmetrical power relations, the cult leader is the one deemed responsible for the problems and pain caused by NRMs. This effectively functions to absolve NRM devotees (and their families) of any responsibility or guilt for their choices. They are the victims of the leader's exploitive and deceptive tactics.

News and entertainment media shape and reflect this common understanding of the cult leader. When cult-related events occur, news headlines and magazine covers emphasize these ideas in their representations of the cult leader. Through still images and descriptions the media paints a picture of what these figures look like – inside and out. Implicit in this coverage is the sense that the cult leaders' dress and appearance communicate something important about them and their beliefs. These images and descriptions circulate across various media reinforcing the cult stereotype, versions of which appear in educational and fictional television programs, as well as film. These visual and sartorial framings – when writing, casting, and dressing cult leader characters – further reinforce the dominant view of cults. In doing so entertainment media weaves together fantasy and entertaining plots with "fragments of historical facts" (Sturken 1997: 32). Historian Anne Hollander argues that "people dress and observe other dressed people with a set of pictures in mind – pictures in a particular style" (1978: 311). When people think cult leader, often a picture or set of pictures come to mind.

The media and visual culture surrounding NRMs often highlights the distinctive style and dress of the groups' leaders; however, it is important to recognize that religious leaders across a variety of traditions don religious garments and observe specific dress practices, especially when performing sacred duties. Catholic priests put on embroidered vestments, Buddhist monks wear simply-made robes, and televangelists sport beautifully-cut suits. Distinct religious clothing separates leaders from ordinary followers and exemplifies their special status as figures who dedicate their lives to spiritual pursuits. Scholar William Keenan explains, "Sacred dress, an icon of holiness, plays an important part in the desexualization of bodies 'consecrated' for divine service" (1999: 389–90). Religious clothing emphasizes the significance of the spiritual office being occupied (priest, monk, pastor) and performed, while diminishing the importance of the individual.

Further, religious dress functions to establish the authority and legitimacy of spiritual leaders (Schmidt 1989: 41; Dwyer-McNulty 2014: 10). This distinct religious clothing often contains symbolic meanings and references to the history of the tradition, which enhances its sense of sacrality. The details – from design and color to fabric and embellishments – matter as they convey spiritual as well as sartorial meanings. These details visually connect religious leaders with theological values and devotional practices and enhance their sacred power. According to Keenan, "religious dress configures the body-self of its wearer at the margin between the sacred and the profane, the holy and the unholy" (1999: 391). As such, it constitutes a powerful way that spiritual leaders proclaim and enact their religious authority.

It should be no surprise then to learn that leaders of NRMs draw on these existing ideas and religious dress traditions to construct their spiritual authority, legitimacy, and charisma (Bromley 2014). However, there is no single distinctive form of dress for leaders of new religions. It is important, then, to recognize the arbitrariness of the cult stereotype and framework. Cult leader clothing only looks different because it is seen through the lens of beliefs in cultic deviance. People expect the Dalai Lama to wear robes and astronauts to wear spacesuits, but when the context shifts and leaders of NRMs utilize distinct forms of dress, they are seen as strange.

Nevertheless, clothing and dress do play an important role in how NRM leaders present themselves and in how they are perceived. There are also some dominant dress patterns in their self-presentation. In what follows I sketch the outlines of a general typology of religious dress utilized by NRM leaders to build their charisma and status. This typology identifies three dominant patterns of religious dress – robes and the monk, the suit and the minister, and the mantle and the king/queen. Each pattern refers to a form of clothing and a religious status often associated with it. No classification scheme is exhaustive or perfect; however, this system provides insights into the significant role of clothing in NRM leadership and a strong foundation of knowledge on which to build.

Robes and the Monk

In 1965, sixty-nine-year-old A. C. Bhaktivedanta Swami Prabhupada (1896–1977) arrived in New York City from India. He came to the United States as a missionary promoting a form of Gaudiya Vaishnava. More specifically, he followed the teachings of Shri Caitanya and devoted himself to Lord Krishna and inspired others to do likewise, primarily through the chanting of the names of God. Prabhupada became the founder of the International Society for Krishna Consciousness (ISKCON), a new religion in the American landscape that gained notoriety and numerous converts in the 1960s and 1970s. By 2007, membership was global and numbered approximately one million (Ketola 2008: 6, 45–50; Karapanagiotis 2021: 29–30).

When Prabhupada arrived "his personal effects consist[ed] of but a few sets of saffron renunciant's cloth, a pair of white rubber shoes, and forty rupees"

(Goswami & Gupta 2005: 81). The simplicity of his material possessions reflected his earlier vow of renunciation to become a sannyasi, a religious ascetic (Olivelle 2003). Outward physical and clothing changes accompanied this inward spiritual commitment. In this case, Prabhupada shaved his head, wore the mark of a Vaishnava on his forehead (tilak), donned simple saffron robes (kurta and dhoti), and carried his bead bag (gomukhi) (Goswami & Gupta 2005: 81). This distinctive form of religious adornment symbolized his humility, freedom from vanity, and surrender to Krishna.

These features characterized Prabhupada's dominant form of dress throughout his leadership of ISKCON (see Figure 1). In one exchange, for example, Prabhupada insisted that "sannyasis must dress in saffron with robes and shaved head" (Kamboj 2018). Pictures of him in the media, on the internet, and in devotees' visions consistently depict him in this manner. For example, in a series of meditations entitled *The Divine Love Trip*, a disciple of Prabhupada shared this description:

> In his left hand Srila Prabhupada held an elegant cane which swung forward, tapping the earth as he walked. In his right hand he carried an effulgent saffron bead bag. On his sacred beads he chanted the Hare Krishna mahamantra, and as he walked the Lord's blessings were in his footsteps. Srila Prabhupada moved around his field in transcendental happiness. His saffron robes blew in the wind making it appear as though he were gliding, and I saw the earth begin to change beneath him. (Dasi 2020)

This meditation emphasizes the connection between Prabhupada's appearance and his spiritual gifts. It draws attention to the significance of the color saffron, important for multiple reasons. It signals the status of sannyasi, represents the sacrifice (Agni) from Vedic times, and symbolizes fire, which brings light, as knowledge burns away ignorance. Prabhupada also carries a gomukhi, a bag to contain his prayer beads (japa mala), which are used to chant the names of God, a central practice in ISKCON. His flowing robes reflect his piety even as he changes the world. Shrines dedicated to Prabhupada also feature him in this attire, sometimes adorned with flowers. Garlands of flowers mark auspicious occasions and persons. They signify a form of respect and recognition of someone's specialness, and the Kadamba flower, which appears in Prabhupada's garlands, has deep associations with Krishna (Ramachandran 2022).

In the 1960s and 1970s, Maharishi Mahesh Yogi (1918–2008) gained widespread popularity in the United States and Europe for his teachings, now known as Transcendental Meditation (TM). He is most recognizable for his spiritual mentoring of the Beatles in 1967, but his popularity peaked in 1975 when he appeared on *The Merv Griffin Show* and attracted celebrities to TM, including Griffin himself and actor Clint Eastwood. Trained by Swami Saraswati, an

Figure 1 A photograph of A.C. Bhaktivedanta Swami Prabhupada taken in Germany, 1974. He is depicted wearing saffron robes, adorned with flower garlands, and holding his bead bag. This attire combined with his meditative pose emphasizes his spiritual insights and intellect. Photo by Christian Jansen, Creative Commons Attribution 3.0

adherent of Advaita Vedanta, Mahesh practiced celibacy, studied the Vedas, and learned the power of meditation. As his spiritual influence grew, he became known as a "great seer," a gift recognized by the title Maharishi, and vowed to bring his teaching – that all could be enlightened – to the world (Humes 2005: 55–79).

Throughout his prominent career, the Maharishi sported long hair and a beard while wearing white silk robes (kurta and dhoti) and saffron prayer beads. His style, dress, and hair set him apart. When asked by interested audiences and potential converts if they should also have long hair, the Maharishi said no. He explained, "I am a monk from the Himalayas and that is why I wear a white robe and have long hair. Eventually I will go back to the Himalayas" (*Montreal*

Gazette 1972). As with Prabhupada, the Maharishi's style reflected his religious status and commitments. The white color of his robes symbolized purity and wisdom and identified those who observed celibacy through discipline of the body and mind. It also highlighted his spiritual lineage and connected him to his teacher Swami Brahmamanda Saraswati, who often wore white. In addition, he regularly sat upon an antelope or deer skin, cared for and positioned by close followers, who also practiced celibacy. According to one contemporary practitioner, if practicing TM outside, the antelope skin protects one from insects and it is also purported to aid meditation by preventing energy from going into the ground (Smith 2022). Photos and videos of his appearances highlight his distinct dress and unique antelope accessory. Taken together, the Maharishi's sartorial style emphasized his spiritual knowledge, special status, and religious authority (For more information about Transcendental Meditation and Maharishi Mahesh Yogi, see Sawyer & Humes 2023.)

Art and written descriptions of him emphasize the power and effect of his appearance. For example, in 1968, after mentioning his practice of celibacy and his undergraduate degree in physics, a newspaper article reported: "Maharishi, a tiny man with flowing black hair and a beard streaked with gray, sat in the lotus position on a deerskin laid upon a red velvet couch in the Plaza Hotel. He wore a white dhoti and his wooden slippers were on the rug before him" (Buck 1968). Similarly, upon arriving in Iowa to visit Maharishi International University, a local newspaper article stated: "Bearded Guru Maharishi Mahesh Yogi, his flowing white silk robes fluttering in the Iowa prairie wind, stepped off a pink chartered plane here Wednesday and received a regal welcome" (*Ames Daily Tribune* 1975). These descriptions, along with photographs and drawings of him, highlight the powerful impression made by his hair and clothing choices (see Figure 2). They help create his mystique and spiritual aura.

Swami Prabhupada and the Maharishi Mahesh Yogi are two of many others, including Swami Satchidananda, Swami Muktananda, and Bhagwan Shree Rajneesh, who wore distinct clothing to signal their religious status (Harvard University). While these dress decisions represent important elements of their respective religious and cultural traditions, they were decoded by observers and adherents within a Western context, one shaped by what scholar Jane Iwamura calls the "Oriental Monk." In her book *Virtual Orientalism* (2011), Iwamura builds on Edward Said's concept of Orientalism, a discourse that has managed and produced the concept of "the Orient" to benefit Western European interests. Said argues that "the relationship between Occident and Orient is a relationship of power, of domination, of varying degrees of a complex hegemony" (Said 1980: 11–13). Iwamura extends Said's analysis to contemporary Western media and popular culture, which often features the figure of the "Oriental Monk." She

Figure 2 A photograph of Maharishi Mahesh Yogi wearing his trademark white robes and prayer beads. He is seated on an animal skin in a meditative pose and holding a bouquet of flowers. His bare feet and sandals highlight his simplicity and humility, while enhancing his spiritual aura. Taken in 1967. Photo courtesy of PictureLux /The Hollywood Archive/Alamy Stock Photo.

writes, "We recognize him as the representative of an otherworldly (though perhaps not entirely alien) spirituality that draws from the ancient wellsprings of 'Eastern' civilization and culture." This homogenizing concept that circulates in American popular culture includes different religious figures, such as gurus, sages, swamis, and masters, from a variety of ethnic backgrounds. Observers and viewers know this religious figure by "his spiritual commitment, his calm demeanor, his Asian face, *his manner of dress*, and – most obviously – his ... gendered character" (Iwamura 2011: 6, emphasis added). Iwamura highlights the ways Orientalist ideas about Asian religions are used to meet Western spiritual desires (Iwamura 2011: 20).

This discursive framework draws attention to the spiritual and symbolic significance of Prabhupada and Maharishi's attire, rather than its regional and historical particularities. Nathan Joseph captures this complexity in his examination of uniforms: "The meaning of clothing is thereby often distorted and subjected to mythmaking or abstraction where the lack of strict congruence between symbol and reality is irrelevant. The result is a sartorial vocabulary of stereotypes, cultural exemplars, and free associations" (1986: 103). For devotees of Prabhupada and the Maharishi, the details and resonances of their hair styles and religious dress mattered. For the media and observers, though, their overall style eclipsed the specifics. They were interpreted through the lens of Iwamura's "Oriental Monk" and defined in large part by a sartorial stereotype that continues to circulate in news headlines, television shows, blockbuster movies, and on the internet.

The Suit and the Minister

While robes have an explicitly religious history, the suit, popularly known now as "the business suit," is often viewed as a secular garment as evidenced by its naming. However, examining the history of the suit reveals strong associations with Protestant Christianity. For example, early in its history, religious Nonconformists in England, including Quakers, as well as John Wesley and his early followers, wore the suit with its "dark and restricted colour palette." This choice of attire represented simplicity and morality, a rejection of ostentatious displays of wealth, pride, and vanity (Breward 2016: 46). In the early nineteenth-century United States, this trend continued. "The minister's black (or dark-colored) suit, free from ornamentation, expensive fabric, and flamboyant color, as well as the conservatively groomed body in it, was intended both to distance Protestant ministers from their Roman Catholic counterparts and to signal the sobriety, unostentatiousness, and propriety of the office" (Payne 2015: 87). By the mid-nineteenth century, though, professionals started donning the suit and its associations with authority and economic success began to emerge and dominate. Ministers continued to wear suits, but by the 1950s a suit worn with a white-collared shirt became the de rigueur attire of businessmen (Sims 2010). These associations with the suit increased with the popular 1975 book *Power Dressing*, which explicitly linked it with wealth, success, and leadership. A number of religious and NRM leaders, including Brigham Young, Marcus Garvey, Charles Fillmore, and Elijah Muhammad, wore suits, and the trend continues today. In this section we focus on two distinctive examples – Father Divine and L. Ron Hubbard.

Father Divine (c.1880–1965), an African American religious leader, established an interracial religious movement, the International Peace Mission, in the early 1900s. Divine, who proclaimed himself to be God, preached a mix of Protestant Christianity and New Thought combined with economic self-help and a rejection of racial categories (Weisenfeld 2016: 78–9). Unity with

Father's "Divine Mind" "would lead to good health, prosperity, and true happiness." Followers lived communally in peace missions across the country and around the world. They pooled resources, bought and renovated properties, and established businesses. In the 1930s, during the hardships of the Great Depression, the Mission provided followers with jobs and affordable food through its entrepreneurial endeavors (Primiano 2017). Historian Jill Watts explains part of his appeal. "Father Divine furnished food, clothing, and shelter to destitute blacks, but also provided a theology that promised a better life and a brighter future to anyone, regardless of economic status. Father Divine personified the Horatio Alger myth, and his success proved that even for blacks, America was a land of opportunity" (Watts 1992: 61).

Given the movement's commitment to living in the Kingdom of Heaven in the here and now combined with Father Divine's godly status, the Peace Mission leader did not shy away from displays of wealth and prosperity. For example, a 1937 newspaper article described the lavish $40,000 "throne car" being built for Divine by a devoted follower. The article detailed its amazing features: "Mounted on a long, expensive chassis (Duesenberg), the car will contain in the rear an elevated plush throne, topped by a ceiling of snow white plush, dotted with gold stars. At each side will be star-shaped windows" (*Windsor Star* 1937). The Mission's Holy Communion Banquets were equally lavish. In 1942, the menu of one featured "no fewer than thirty vegetables, forty-five meats, fifteen relishes, fourteen breads, and fifteen deserts" (Lindsey 2014: 368). Divine's financial success functioned as a visual and tangible affirmation of his message.

Father Divine's dress and general appearance also reinforced his heavenly position and teachings (see Figures 3 and 4). In photographs, Divine typically appears wearing a suit complete with white-collared shirt, silk tie, pocket square, two pens, a boutonniere, and gold lapel pins. An early history of the movement emphasized the expense and luxury that surrounded him. "He rides around in a Cadillac driven by his private chauffeur and wears custom-made suits and the finest haberdashery" (Harris 1953: 12). While his suits recalled the standard attire of Protestant ministers, their varied colors (blue, gray, pin-striped), gleaming fabrics, and custom tailoring, as well as the accompanying gold accessories, indicated status, success, and wealth. In 1937, one newspaper article noted that he wore a "blue suit, shirt and tie, with a gold insignia on the lapel of his coat and two fountain pens and a gold pencil stuck in the breast pocket of his coat" (*Oakland Tribune* 1937). In December 1950, Father and the second Mother Divine appeared on the cover of *Ebony*. The young Mother Divine, wearing an elegant dress with a lace overlay, looks adoringly up at Father Divine, who sports a dark suit, rosebud boutonniere (symbolic of the

Figure 3 Father Divine wearing a stylish three-piece suit and white fedora as he sits in the back of a vehicle as part of a parade in 1938. Photo courtesy of Bettman/Getty Images.

movement's Rosebud Choir), abstract printed silk tie, and a few gold pins (see Figure 4). The accompanying article, entitled "Life with Father," describes their spiritual and celibate union and includes a photograph of Divine standing next to a dresser full of clothes, including numerous collared shirts, handkerchiefs, and ties. The caption states: "Private suite is maintained for Father Divine in missions in every city he is likely to visit. Each has a supply of fresh shirts, socks, ties, underwear, pajamas. Photo of Mother Divine is on dresser wherever he sleeps" (Divine 1950). The photographs and descriptions emphasize Divine's extravagant lifestyle and his position of power.

Divine's stunning suits and elegant style affirmed his celestial status and demonstrated the powerful and tangible implications of his message. He was God, but also an example of what his followers could attain (Weisenfeld 2016: 78). Beyond its impact on his followers and the movement, Divine's visual and sartorial rhetoric simultaneously accepted and rejected dominant norms of the

Figure 4 Cover of *Ebony* December 1950. The cover features an elegantly dressed Mother Divine gazing up at Father Divine wearing a beautiful suit and tie. ©1950. EBONY. All Rights reserved. Used with permission.

time. Wearing a suit, as opposed to robes or vestments, positioned Divine and his work in the visual culture of Protestant ministers. In this way, the suit worked to diminish the perceived danger and foreignness of his theology. It also recalled the long-standing Black Church tradition of dressing up for worship by wearing one's "Sunday Best." This practice, embraced by Black men and women, simultaneously showed their deep commitment to God, displayed their spiritual identities, and afforded the pleasure of cultivating an empowering aesthetic (O'Neal 1999: 125–6; Beckford 2009: 135–51; Pinn 2009: 7–8). Moreover, the suit distanced Divine's body and persona from racist stereotypes that characterized Black men as dangerous or buffoons (Dorman 1988). It also aligned him with dominant white notions about respectability and success, civilization and sophistication. This is not to say that the suit protected Divine from persecution, allegations, and racism. It did not (Weisenfeld 2016: 83–4). However, given the prominence of negative stereotypes about cults and about Black people in the early twentieth century, Divine's choice to wear custom-made suits and silk ties matters.

L. Ron Hubbard (1911–1986) was another prominent NRM leader who regularly wore a suit on official occasions, including giving lectures and interviews, touring to promote his message, and posing for portraits. After his book *Dianetics* (1950) met with great success, he founded Scientology, a movement dedicated to helping people eliminate negative memories and realize their full potential. Amid the mental health crisis of the 1940s and 1950s, Hubbard's science of the mind and auditing rituals offered people answers to their problems for a fee. Even after his death, the movement continues to revolve around Hubbard and his works. Scholar Dorthe Refslund Christensen writes, "he is the only ultimate source and legitimizing resource of the religious and therapeutic claims of the church" (2005: 28). His centrality is such that Scientology Centers honor his legacy through offices dedicated to and reserved for him.

While insiders and outsiders debate accounts of Hubbard's childhood, looking at hagiographies of his background help us understand how his followers see him and want others to view him. These accounts emphasize Hubbard's exceptional childhood, including his ability to read and write at a young age, his learning from Blackfoot Indians, and his early achievement of Eagle Scout status. As a young man, he served in the US Naval Reserves, was mentored by a student of Sigmund Freud, and researched science and religion through extensive reading and travel. Unhappy with current answers to life's problems, Hubbard developed his own experiments, ideas, and theories (Christensen 2005). According to followers, these vast and exotic experiences set Hubbard apart and became the basis for *Dianetics* and later Scientology. (For more information about Hubbard and Scientology, see Westbrook 2022.)

Posed photographs of and interviews with Hubbard (prior to his going into seclusion in 1975) typically show Hubbard seated at a desk wearing a suit and white-collared shirt along with a tie or ascot. These images evoke the dominant associations of the suit with business acumen and leadership. The selection of the ascot, neckwear often associated with British elites attending horse races at Royal Ascot, highlights Hubbard's cosmopolitan experiences. The ascot might

Figure 5 L. Ron Hubbard wearing suit and tie while seated at desk holding feather pen. The bookcase in the background and desk accessories enhance his intellectual and professional appearance. Taken in 1960. Photo courtesy of Mondadori Portfolio/Getty Images.

also be a subtle nod to Hubbard's naval past as it is part of full-dress uniforms worn for ceremonial occasions. In addition to these sartorial choices, Hubbard consistently appears at a desk with bookshelves or artwork in the background with a serious and thoughtful look on his face. In one often utilized image, he is holding a feather pen (see Figure 5) and paused in the act of writing and in another his gaze is directed upward.

Hubbard's sartorial and setting choices reinforce hagiographical accounts of his life and his work. He appears successful, world-wise, and intellectual – a combination of businessman and professor. He represents the individual possibilities promised by Scientology – a visual reminder of the movement's theology. Photographs of him in his suit conducting experiments on plants strengthen these impressions (see Figure 6). These posed photographs take on added resonance as newspaper coverage focused on *Dianetics* and the scandals associated with Hubbard but did not often describe what he looked like or include photos of him. This shows how Hubbard and Scientology protected and controlled his image and the ways "L. Ron Hubbard and Scientology have always been and will, most probably, always be inseparable" (Christensen 2005: 227).

While the robes worn by Prabhupada and the Maharishi tapped into Orientalist discourse about the wisdom to be gained from Asian religious figures, the suit evoked equally salient associations with leadership, authority, success, and legitimacy that reinforced the power claimed and exercised by

Figure 6 L. Ron Hubbard wearing a suit while conducting plant-based research in the greenhouse of his Sussex mansion in 1972. Photo courtesy of Keystone Press/Alamy Stock Photo.

NRM leaders. The suit functioned as a material affirmation of their teachings. Father Divine's claims to divinity and prosperity could be seen in his custom-made suits and luxurious surroundings, while Hubbard's suit-wearing combined with his posing in educational settings reflected his teachings about a science of the mind and the success possible through Scientology. Further, given the distinctive economic arrangements in both movements (communalism in the Peace Mission and the fees charged for auditing and advancing within Scientology), the business connotations of the suit reinforced their financial ideas. The suit aligned with and strengthened their claims to both spiritual and economic wisdom. In addition, the suit set leaders apart from followers – it highlighted their unique places in their respective movements – even as it likened them to Protestant ministers who wore suits. Although the media and outsiders criticized Divine and Hubbard, and their unorthodox theologies, these men continued to present themselves as respectable, according to dominant ideas regarding dress. However, such sartorial claims to religious respectability did not protect Divine or Hubbard from criticism and controversy. For critics of these movements, their attire evoked the old biblical notion found in Matthew 7:15: Beware of a wolf in sheep's clothing. Respectable dress did not automatically mean respectable theology. It was an important reminder that the deception associated with charismatic cult leaders occurred at all levels, the sartorial and spiritual, the financial and the theological.

Mantle and Crown, Kings and Queens

As with the patterns of leadership attire already examined, the use of royal dress has precedents in the broader religious landscape. Notably, papal vestments recall two of the most notable sartorial symbols of royalty – the mantle and the crown. The pope, Bishop of Rome and leader of the Roman Catholic Church, has historically worn elaborate vestments, and until 1964, wore the triregnum, a papal tiara made up of three golden crowns embellished with precious gems (see Figure 7; Tribe 2023). This attire represented and reinforced the pope's status "as God's representative on earth," and as one scholar explains, it functioned as a "symbol of his power, articulating his equal status with royalty" (Hume 2013: 13–34). Until the 1700s in Europe, this equation of royal and clerical power was codified in sumptuary laws. For example, in England, laws restricted the wearing of desirable furs to "the aristocratic and clerical elite" (Emberley 2010). Such laws also reserved certain colors, such as purple and gold, and fabrics, including damask and taffeta, for royalty only. This not only created distinct forms of royal dress but also made social status visible.

Similarly, the use of the royal mantle and crown by NRM leaders emphasizes their special role and claims to power. In the nineteenth century, Mormon James Strang (1813–1856) claimed to be appointed by Joseph Smith (1805–1844) as his successor. Strang led his followers to Beaver Island, Michigan, and in 1850 proclaimed himself king of his church in a coronation ceremony. According to accounts, Strang sat on a throne and was "cloaked in a faux-ermine-trimmed red flannel cape, and a mural of a palace exterior hung behind him" (Edwards 2009; Blythe 2014). In the twentieth century, Yahweh ben Yahweh (1935–2007), the founder of the Nation of Yahweh in Florida, was increasingly described in terms of royalty and wore white robes and a white turban (his crown) to symbolize this status. And in France, Gilbert Bourdin (1923–1998), the founder of Mandarom, wore a mantle and crowned himself "the Cosmoplanetary Messiah" (Palmer & Gareau 2017). In this part, we will look at two examples that provide different insights and perspectives on this pattern. First, Rev. Sun Myung Moon, founder of the Unification movement, an international NRM that sparked the brainwashing controversy in the United States, wore royal garb during ceremonial occasions. Second, Ruth Norman, known as Uriel, who became the leader of the California-based Unarius Academy of Science in 1971, and Queen of Archangels in 1973, regularly wore the attire of royalty.

Figure 7 Portrait of Pope Pius X (1835–1914) wearing embroidered vestments and a papal tiara, sometimes referred to as a triple crown. The three levels of the tiara highlight the pope's roles as "father of kings, governor of the world, and Vicar of Christ on earth" (Tribe 2023). Portrait courtesy of Chronicle/Alamy Stock Photo.

The Korean-born Moon (1920–2012) converted to Christianity as a child and had subsequent revelations of the unique role he would play in fulfilling Christian prophecy. In the 1950s he founded the Holy Spirit Association for the Unification of World Christianity, dedicated to bringing Christianity together under his leadership. Soon the movement began sending missionaries to Europe and the United States, and its following in America increased in the 1970s after Moon and his second wife Hak Ja Han (b. 1943) emigrated. As the movement's theology unfolded, Moon declared that he and his wife were the True Parents of humankind and later "we are the Savior, the Lord of the Second Advent, the Messiah" (Bromley & Cowan 2015: 84–7). Along with this special spiritual status, Moon led the movement to economic success. It owns the

Washington Times, True World Foods, and more. Further, the movement's political conservatism and monetary donations made it a player on the Washington, DC scene. For example, the movement supported President Richard Nixon and Lt. Col. Oliver North, as well as financially helping Jerry Falwell's Liberty University. Former Vice President Dan Quayle attended Moon's eightieth birthday celebration (Cowan & Bromley 2015: 78–98).

Within the development of the movement, Moon often wore two kinds of attire – conservative business suits for speaking engagements, world tours, and festivals; and royal garb for ceremonial occasions, notably for the performance of the Blessing, mass arranged marriages involving hundreds and sometimes thousands of couples (Wadler 1982). In this ritual, Moon and his wife would wed and bless the selected couples who then became spiritual children of these True Parents, part of their "God-centered" royal lineage (Cowan & Bromley 2015: 87–9). As early as 1962, Moon wore long light-colored robes and a crown-like headpiece, while his wife wore light-colored robes and no crown, during a Blessing ritual. In photographs from a Blessing ceremony in 1969, both are wearing white and gold robes and crowns (Sunhak Institute of History). This trend continued in subsequent decades. In a 1970 newspaper article, Moon and his wife were described as wearing "golden robes and crowns" (*The Post Standard*) and in 1982, a description stated, "Clad in flowing white robes with white, crown-like headgear, the Moons stood on pedestals" (*Miami Herald*). The wearing of mantle and crown highlights Moon's divine status and the marriage ritual's centrality in the movement (see Figure 8). Marriage, as one scholar described it, is "the major turning point in the individual member's growth toward spiritual perfection." It frees devotees from sin, incorporates them into Moon's spiritual family, and empowers them "to realize a God-centered family" (Grace 1985: 114). This family unit, then, forms the basis for building the Kingdom of God, led by the regally dressed Moon. (For more information about Unificationism, see Mickler 2022.)

Rev. Moon and his wife also donned mantle and crown on March 23, 2004 (see Figure 9). On this day, at the Dirksen Senate Office Building in Washington, DC, members of Congress and over 200 guests gathered for an "Ambassadors of Peace" event organized by the Unification movement. After honoring the awardees, the event shifted into the "Crown of Peace" ceremony, a coronation of Rev. and Mrs. Moon. According to the Unification movement, in this event the "True Parents were crowned before all humanity because they fulfilled their responsibility to unify all races and religions and launch the movement of Peace to heal the world. They were crowned as King and Queen of the Second and Third Israel." Photos of the event show them being presented with luxurious red mantles embroidered with gold designs and large gold

Wearing Their Faith 21

Figure 8 Rev. and Mrs. Moon wearing royal robes and crowns, as well as floral boutonnieres, at a Blessing ceremony in South Korea, 2002. Photo courtesy of Young Jae-Wook/AFP via Getty Images.

Figure 9 Rev. and Mrs. Moon attired in red, royal mantles with gold trim and embellishments, as well as red and gold crowns. Taken at the Ambassadors of Peace Ceremony in 2004, in the Dirksen Senate Office Building. Screenshot by author of writer Andrew Cusack's critical coverage of the event (2004).

crowns. Surrounded by the symbols of American political power, Moon demonstrated his own equal or greater power and claim to authority (Gorenfeld 2004; Stolberg 2004).

Royal garb functions in multiple ways during Blessing ceremonies and the coronation event. It highlights the couple's special theological status – it sets the Moons apart from followers and other religious and political leaders. Further, during ritual events, royal garb emphasizes their authority and legitimacy – their power to bring men and women together, bless their unions, and extend the movement's spiritual lineage. It also emphasizes how this power extends beyond religious ideals (narrowly defined) to other arenas of life, including family, media, business, and politics. The juxtaposition of a royally dressed Rev. and Mrs. Moon in US Senate offices in front of a photograph of the Capitol Building disrupts ideas about separation of church and state, as well as conceptions of religion as "private." For critics, it fuels fears that Moon and his movement seek political power and control that threaten democracy and freedom of religion.

While much less well known, Ruth Norman (1900–1993) became the sole leader of the Unarius Academy of Science in 1971, after the passing of her husband. In the movement's "new science of life" (members do not consider it a religion), Norman, viewed as an advanced channel and psychic clairvoyant, communicated with and conveyed the teachings of the Spiritual Masters, beings such as Abraham, Jesus, and Muhammad, who now live on the non-physical Inner Planes where their ideas have continued to advance and develop. Norman also shared insights and knowledge gained from her numerous past lives (Calvert 2024). From these teachings, followers (known as students) learn about "the continuity of life" and pursue "spiritual growth and healing" (Tumminia 2005: 7; Calvert 2024). Norman's authority increased in 1973 when she became attuned to an advanced spiritual being named Uriel – a transformation symbolized by the changing of Norman's name to Uriel and her donning the attire of royalty (see Figure 10). Scholar Diana Tumminia notes, "In her persona as Uriel, Ruth Norman always appeared costumed. She wore specially made, floor-length gowns, capes, elaborate wigs, and tiaras. She carried a royal staff or scepter and sometimes a bouquet of roses" (2005: 55).

Many of Uriel's outfits, as we can see in Figure 11, reflected the visual vocabulary of royalty (mantle, crown, scepter), a sartorial choice that emphasized her attainment of a higher spiritual pathway and her past lives as a spiritual leader (Calvert 2024). To some observers, elements of Norman's royal costumes, specifically gowns made of metallic fabrics that included dramatic structural elements, such as elaborate Elizabethan standing collars and strands of lights, recalled space-inspired designs (Brownie 2019). However, to Uriel and her students, the brilliant colors and sparkly fabrics helped attune them to the indescribable beauty, radiance,

Wearing Their Faith 23

Figure 10 Uriel in lavender gown with dramatic hood and deep purple trim. She holds a scepter and wears a tiara of stars. Photo courtesy of Unarius Academy of Science.

Figure 11 Uriel holding a scepter and wearing a golden crown-like headpiece along with gold robes. Worn during a psychodrama on the rise and fall of Lemuria. Photo courtesy of Unarius Academy of Science.

and light that characterizes the Inner Planes, a non-physical dimension of existence (Calvert 2024). Uriel herself said in one interview, "In the inner worlds, we wear much color, many things that are radiant" (Warner 1979), while another source stated, "her dress style imitated the fashion of extraterrestrials, whose attire was brighter and more radiant than any clothing on Earth" (Palmer & Gareau 2017). The overall effect was that of a radiant queen, a look that simultaneously showcased her unique abilities and her desire to help her students.

Uriel's use of royal dress and other costumes also played a pivotal role in the movement's psychodramas, improvisational re-enactments of past lives, that aided students on their spiritually progressive pathway. During these re-enactments, Uriel's costumes functioned as a visible reminder of those memories and times. "The outfits were not only thrilling to look at, they served a purpose. Like the costumes worn in historical dramas, the outfits Uriel wore helped recreate what life was like during the students' previous incarnations" (Lodi 2016). Costumes, as a part of these psychodramas, helped students overcome "fears, shocks, and blocks" from past lives. Further, Uriel chose to wear costumes that she thought would be the most helpful for her students (Calvert 2024). In addition, given that Uriel designed many of her costumes (which were then made by students), she selected fabrics, styles, and embellishments that would create resonance and assist her students and other viewers with "attunement" to their higher selves and the higher Spiritual Masters (Unarius Academy of Science 2020; Calvert 2024). The same sartorial intentionality and authority can be seen in the movement's videos. In one drama Uriel appears in the heavens wearing a sparkly gown and crown beckoning a seeker to "come with me through this tunnel of stars," and at another point in the video, she is seated in a gold wingback chair wearing a gold gown and large crown ("Creativity for AVAM"). Uriel's appearance as royalty emphasized her enlightened spiritual state, her connection to other planes of reality, and her desire to help others.

While wearing the business suit aligned male NRM leaders with dominant dress norms, donning mantles and crowns, as with robes, set both men and women apart, especially in the American context. For example, Uriel's regal attire combined with her message attracted attention and publicity to the movement. She garnered news coverage and appeared on different TV shows, including the reality show *Real People* (no date) and *The David Letterman Show* (1982–1991). Uriel often appears as the butt of the joke in these programs and in news coverage, past and present. One journalist stated, "Uriel looked like Endora from Bewitched crossed with Glinda the Good Witch – a septuagenarian goddess in glittery gowns and candy-colored wigs" (Lodi 2016). Nevertheless, Uriel utilized these platforms to share her message at the national level, the same way she and her followers did through the performances they aired on local access television. For Rev. Moon, the events where he wore mantle and crown received ample and often negative media coverage. In these instances, Moon's regal attire heightened people's long-standing concerns about the movement, including his seemingly autocratic power over his followers and his desires to extend his power into so-called nonreligious realms. Beyond the publicity and perceptions of them, wearing mantle and crown highlighted the unparalleled status that Moon and Uriel occupied in their respective movements. They are clearly at the top, endowed with unique and inspired authority.

Conclusion

This section has analyzed the central role clothing plays in the creation and maintenance of NRM leadership. Whether robes, suit, or mantle, these clothing choices help construct the charismatic leader's status, authority, and legitimacy within their respective movements. This attire constitutes a vital way that leadership is exercised and maintained. Charisma, one of the primary traits often associated with NRM leaders, is not an inherent gift, but rather a relational concept between "believers (or followers) and the man [or woman] in whom they believe" (Wilson 1975: 7). As such, it takes work. Scholar Diana Tumminia conceptualizes these practices as "charismatic labor," by which she means the work that leaders (and followers) perform to maintain "the perception of the extraordinary qualities of that leader" (2005: 51). Utilizing this concept, we can see how what I am calling the "dress work" performed by NRM leaders helps them establish and maintain their elevated positions. By dressing in particular ways, they not only embody central theological teachings and values, but also meet "cultural or subcultural understanding[s] of what constitutes charisma" in these movements (Tumminia 2005: 52). Followers, then, work to affirm and share these understandings with others through a variety of practices, such as writing poems, sharing testimonies, and making devotional art, that highlight the special qualities of their leader. We have seen examples of these practices in this section, and we might consider other actions, such as sourcing fabric, making garments, laundering clothes, and caring for them, as additional forms of charismatic labor performed by followers (Tumminia 2005: 52). Thus, rather than seeing dress as a superficial, yet interesting, facet of cult leader life, we can recognize the powerful way clothing practices generate and sustain support for NRM leadership.

In thinking about the dress and charismatic labor of cult leaders, more research needs to be done. We need to investigate more fully the power and function of accessories. Consider how accessories, such as hats and sunglasses, complete a look. Father Divine often wore hats with his custom-made suits, and L. Ron Hubbard sometimes wore a navy dress cap (or a variation on one) in his more casually posed photographs. Hats also figured prominently in the attire of NRM leaders we have not examined in this section. For example, Elijah Muhammad, Prophet of the Nation of Islam, wore a black velvet kofia decorated with stars and crescent moon (a symbol of Islam) made of precious gems and metals, including diamonds and platinum (see Figure 12). The history, symbolism, and function of these different headcoverings would be a fruitful area for further study. In thinking about accessories, we might also ask: What shoes did they wear? Did they carry a briefcase or a cane? Sunglasses (or tinted glasses), worn by NRM leaders such as Jim Jones and David Koresh, are another accessory worth further consideration. In the US context, given the importance of eye contact and associations of the eyes with conceptions of transparency and authenticity, obscuring the eyes takes on added significance. Moreover, jewelry, a form of adornment with historical religious resonances, frequently carries powerful symbolic meanings. Jewelry often reflects the heritage and traditions of the movement and can represent someone's status as a leader or member of that group. Jewelry can also have spiritual functions, such as protection from harm (amulet) or amplifying spiritual gifts (talisman). Lastly, we need to think more fully about the significance of hair and the hairstyles worn by NRM leaders. Sociologist Anthony Synnott argues that "hair is perhaps our most powerful symbol of individual and group identity" (1987: 381). Examining these accessories in more depth will provide additional insights into and understanding of how NRM leaders foster and sustain their positions.

Figure 12 Photograph of the Prophet Elijah Muhammad wearing a black velvet kofia adorned with the crescent and star symbol of Islam on a field of bejeweled stars. Taken in Chicago, 1975. Photo courtesy of CPA Media Pte Ltd/Alamy Stock Photo.

The dress work performed by NRM leaders illuminates the importance of material culture in studying NRMs. Scholar David Morgan challenges us to consider how "materiality mediates belief" and to develop a "more capacious account of it, one that looks to the embodied, material features of lived religion." Clothing functions as a vital way that cult leaders "enable and enact" their beliefs, while creating a shared imaginary and aesthetic norms for their followers (Morgan 2010: 12, 7). Through robes, suits, mantles, and crowns, we can see how they create their charismatic aura and embody their beliefs. Such labor is not limited to leaders and in the next section, we examine the ways NRM members do their own dress work and live their beliefs through the selection, wearing, and display of clothing.

2 Dress and the Devotion of NRM Followers

In 1998, the Simpson family – Homer, Marge, Lisa, Bart, and little Maggie – left the First Church of Springfield and joined the Movementarians. They moved to the compound, harvested lima beans, and swapped their usual suburban attire for long, gray robes – the standard uniform of rank-and-file Movementarian members. In 2008, in the series *Monk*, protagonist Adrian Monk is temporarily lured into the Siblings of the Sun in an episode entitled "Mr. Monk Joins a Cult." The group and Monk's temporary allegiance are marked by distinct apparel – women wear yellow sundresses, men wear yellow button-down shirts, and the choir wears yellow robes. And in 2016, promotional images for Hulu's cult-themed show *The Path* depict followers dressed in pure white apparel raising their hands in praise along with their white-clad leader. The television message is clear – cult members wear distinctive and peculiar clothing.

These depictions shape and reflect the hegemonic cult stereotype. While this framing portrays the cult leader as power hungry and deceptive, as discussed in Section 1, it simultaneously promotes ideas about cult converts. For instance, it asserts that those who join cults are weak, gullible, exploited, and likely brainwashed. They are the victims of the cult leaders' machinations. In the circulation of these ideas, the visualization of standardized cult dress in news and entertainment media functions as evidence of their exploitation. Rather than embracing their individuality through the cultivation of unique styles, cult members' lack of autonomy can be seen in their adhering to dress codes and wearing uniform-like apparel. According to this logic, because they all look the same, they must think the same, which means they have been brainwashed by the evil cult leader and his deceptive recruitment tactics. The stereotype essentializes and fixes a few characteristics, including standardized apparel, which homogenizes converts and prevents questioning this interpretive framework (Hall 1997: 257).

This conceptualization focuses on the strange and deviant dress of devotees; however, it neglects the important role that distinct forms of dress play in many groups deemed legitimate religions. Christians often dress up in their "Sunday Best" for church services and outside of services some sport T-shirts with messages featuring religious slogans, such as "Pumpkin Spice and Jesus Christ" and "Fall for Jesus, He Never Leaves." In Orthodox Judaism, men wear yarmulkes during prayers, and some choose to wear them on a daily basis to indicate their religious commitments. And the Amish and Mennonite wear plain dress, simple and modest styles associated with the past. In these contexts and others, wearing distinct religious clothing may result in some eye-rolling and judgments about religious conservativism, but it does not activate the same negative ideas about victimization and brainwashing – with the exception of Islam. (For more information on Islam and veiling, see Alvi, Hoodfar, & McDonough 2003 and Piela 20021).

Dress constitutes an important part of religious life and communities. First, clothing often identifies membership, status, and boundaries. Scholar Kelly J. Baker writes, "Dress has historically functioned for mainstream, utopian, and sectarian religious groups to identify inclusion and roles in a religious community as well as to reify boundaries of a community" (Baker 2008). This community creation and boundary maintenance works in two ways. It reinforces group religious identity, while also signaling this distinctiveness to those outside the group (Entwistle 2000: 51). Second, the clothing of a religious group "may express its hopes, fears, beliefs about the world and the things in it" (Barnard 1996: 18). By examining the clothing choices and contexts of religious groups, we can see what their clothing communicates and the meanings it generates. Third, for individuals, wearing religious dress can function in multiple ways. It can show religious identity to others, reinforce your connections to the tradition, remind you of a religious experience, and protect you from harm (McDannell 1995: 206–12). Fourth, according to scholars of material religion, material objects, including clothing, do not simply provide a glimpse into religious thought, they mediate and constitute religious belief (Morgan 2010: 11–12).

Despite the ways the cult stereotype emphasizes how these groups differ from so-called legitimate religions, clothing functions similarly whether the group in question is labeled a religion or a cult. This demonstrates once again the arbitrariness of this framing as what appears normal in one context is labeled deviant in another. Further, it is important to realize that many NRMs do not adopt distinct forms of religious dress. The members of Peoples Temple wore the typical clothes of their era, as did the Branch Davidians. Therefore, keep in mind that to study the clothing and dress practices of NRMs is to study religion more broadly.

This section examines three NRMs in which clothing plays a significant role. These case studies illuminate the dress work that goes into forming devoted NRM followers. It highlights how clothing helps these groups create identity, cohesion, and distinction. While clothing functions similarly across these groups, we see in these examples how distinct attire can be utilized for varying periods of time and for different religious purposes. Examining the sackcloth vigils of the Children of God (COG) shows the strategic and short-term use of clothing to confront capitalist and Christian systems, while Latter Day Saint (LDS) Elder missionary attire emphasizes the occupational role these young men hold for two years. Finally, the Nation of Islam (NOI) dress code for women challenges stereotypes and infuses women's lives with spiritual meaning. These case studies emphasize how dress functions within particular communities, while simultaneously sending a message to the broader society. Each of these movements utilizes clothing to navigate, confront, and/or challenge stereotypes and assumptions (Palmer & Gareau 2017). Through these examples we can see the important ways that dress work contributes to the creation and maintenance of NRMs.

The Children of God and a Sackcloth Strategy

NRMs utilize religious dress to foster their communities and uphold their theological values, while simultaneously challenging societal norms and misconceptions. Sometimes this challenge is implicit, at other times it is explicit (Palmer & Gareau 2017). The latter is the case with the Children of God (now known as The Family International). Founded in the 1960s in Huntington Beach, California by David "Moses" Berg, the COG successfully recruited youth from the counterculture. Blending elements of the Hippie movement, such as its critiques of established authority and emphasis on authenticity, with the ethics of Evangelical Protestantism (no alcohol, drugs, tobacco, or premarital sex) and his unique scriptural interpretations, Berg's loyal youth followed him and his unfolding message as they traveled around the country (Pountain & Robbins 2000: 76–9; Cowan & Bromley 2015: 101–4). In the late 1960s, the group's message emphasized personal salvation and apocalyptic beliefs combined with criticisms of American capitalism and orthodox Christianity, which he referred to as Churchianity (Van Zandt 1991: 33–4). While the group eventually became infamous for Berg's introduction of unorthodox sexual practices (Flirty Fishing and the Law of Love) (Chancellor 2000: 94–150), during this period of their history, evangelism and eschatology dominated their public image. (For more information about the Children of God/The Family International, see Borowik 2023.)

In some ways, the role of clothing in the movement was unremarkable. The COG had no day-to-day dress code. As one reporter noted, "Most of the girls choose to wear the long, colorful pioneer-type dresses; but they may wear short dresses or jeans. No one appears to be going all-out to look any certain way. A few of the fellows have mustaches or beards; most have only slightly shaggy locks" (Fischer 1971). A former member recalled that the group "looked like gypsies and also like hippies," while noting that some wore "army field jackets and boots," while others "wore berets" (Cooke). Their everyday attire resembled that of the era and the counterculture from which so many of them came.

However, in the late 1960s the movement sought to promote its criticisms of "Churchianity" – inauthentic Christian faith focused on church attendance rather than true commitment – and the American nation by strategically deploying religiously inspired dress to enact their faith and draw attention to their cause. A sense of urgency fueled this strategy as the group feared and felt compelled to warn others of God's impending judgment. They found scriptural support for their apocalyptic views and spiritual attire in the biblical book of Jeremiah. Two passages garnered special attention: Jeremiah 6:26 "O daughter of my people, gird thee with sackcloth, and wallow thyself in ashes: make thee mourning, as for an only son, most bitter lamentation: for the spoiler shall suddenly come upon us," and Jeremiah 7:20 "Therefore thus saith the Lord God: Behold, mine anger and my fury shall be poured out upon this place, upon man, upon beast, and upon the trees of the field, and upon the fruit of the ground; and it shall burn, and shall not be quenched." For Berg and his followers, these verses signaled God's imminent judgment of Churchianity and the United States, as well as the group's special role in upending and revolutionizing both.

These verses describe the disastrous consequences of turning away from God. Berg saw this betrayal of Christianity unfolding at the national level. He interpreted the death of Senate Minority Leader Everett Dirksen in 1969, as part of these apocalyptic events. Deborah Davis, born Linda Berg and the eldest daughter of David Berg and first wife Jane Miller, remembers that for her father, Dirksen's death "was symbolic of the death of the nation, because the senator had tried to pass legislation that would allow mandated prayer and Bible-reading in public schools" (1984). Dirksen disagreed with the Supreme Court's ruling in *Engel v. Vitale* (1962), which determined that school-sponsored prayer was a violation of the Establishment Clause in the US Constitution. In response, he sought a constitutional amendment that would allow school administrators "to permit voluntary prayer but prohibit them from prescribing the form or content of the prayer" (Kyvig 2002: 75). To Berg and his followers, Dirksen's unsuccessful efforts and death epitomized the nation's refusal to "turn back" to God.

In response, while Dirksen lay in state, approximately seventy-five members of the COG held silent vigils at the Capitol Building and the White House. Participants in the vigil walked in unison, thumping their seven-foot staves, while clothed in long red sackcloth (burlap) robes with wooden yokes around their necks and ashes on their foreheads. Once positioned, participants unrolled large scrolls featuring Bible verses warning of God's judgment on the nation(s), including Jeremiah 4:6-7, Psalm 9:17, and Isaiah 60:12. At set times, they "lifted the staffs, and yelled 'Woe' or 'Abomination'" (Van Zandt 1991: 35). However, during most of the vigil, members remained silent, and their attire combined with the scrolls did the speaking for them (Davis 1984).

For the COG their religiously inspired clothing and accessories harkened back to the Bible and carried deep spiritual meaning. Jeremiah 6 described wearing sackcloth and ashes and other passages provided additional inspiration. According to Deborah Davis, "the long robes symbolized mourning for the nation, and the red sackcloth was an ominous sign of the blood that would be shed at the coming destruction. The yokes represented the bondage that was to befall America, paralleling the bondage of the Israelites under the Babylonians" (1984). Male participants sported beards and grew their hair long making them look like ancient Israelites, while women wore large gold or silver earrings (Davis 1984; Van Zandt 1991: 35). Another newspaper interviewee echoed Davis's interpretation and added that the staves symbolized "God's judgment" and that "the wearing of one earring shows 'we're a slave of love to Jesus Christ'" (an interpretation of Deuteronomy 15:17) (Dart 1970). The group repeated vigils at different symbolic sites and events around the country, including Philadelphia (Independence Hall), New York City (Times Square), Chicago (site of the Chicago Seven Trial), and more (Dart 1970).

This distinctive attire constituted a vital part of the vigils and functioned in multiple ways. First, it fostered commitment and unity within the community itself. Planning and purpose characterized the group's clothing, accessories, and actions. Davis recalled that they practiced for hours to achieve their unified march. Further, as can be seen in Figure 13, the creation and curation of their religiously inspired dress required a significant investment of the group's time. They had to work to create these cohesive looks. Second, the symbolism of their attire reflected and reinforced their apocalyptic theology. Members of the group evangelized others in their regular street clothes; however, the vigils required dress work. They aligned their attire with scriptural interpretation, they created a form of religious dress, and in wearing the garments they became "Prophets of Doom." Third, these practices reinforced the idea of authenticity so important to the counterculture and the COG. Both movements wanted to strip away layers of tradition and uncover, in their view, more authentic and therefore meaningful

Figure 13 Children of God wearing sackcloth and ashes while they hold staves and scrolls featuring biblical verses warning of God's impending judgment. Taken in Los Angeles in 1970. Photo courtesy of Los Angeles Times Photographic Archive, UCLA Library Digital Collections. Creative Commons Attribution 4.0 International

experiences (Pountain & Robbins 2000: 76–9). Going to the Bible as a source for their dress inspiration and then handcrafting and curating their vigil attire framed this process as an authentic and powerful way to embody their beliefs. It also implicitly indicted other Christians for their seemingly inauthentic and store-bought performance of Churchianity. Through this strategic sartorial practice, the COG claimed spiritual authority.

In some ways this strategy worked. Through their attire, COG members in the vigils differentiated themselves from the broader society. These were not your typical Sunday-only Christians, and they stood out, which captured media attention (SMU Jones Film 1973). News articles spent precious column space on in-depth descriptions of members' attire and its symbolic spiritual significance. This attention, in turn, further reinforced the movement's theology. Davis likened the vigils to "playing a role in a movie" and called them "great fun," but more than that, the press coverage affirmed the group's sense of mission. "So much attention made us feel important – as if we *actually were* God's endtime prophets, *confirming* what my dad had been telling us" (1984; emphasis added). Davis emphasizes how the clothing, vigil, theology, and media coverage worked together to enliven the group's religious worldview.

While the vigils were unsuccessful in upending Churchianity or American capitalism, their example illustrates how NRMs and religions more broadly can utilize clothing in short-term, strategic ways that explicitly challenge the dominant culture. While dress codes and modesty constitute important themes in examining NRMs and clothing as we will see in the subsequent case studies, COG's sackcloth vigils remind us that dress work can take various forms and be deployed for specific moments and purposes. The COG also draw our attention to the power of clothing to animate a religion's theology and therefore the movement itself.

LDS Elder Missionary Dress and Camouflage Clothing

Unlike the COG, other NRMs, such as the Church of Jesus Christ of Latter-Day Saints (LDS), more subtly navigate societal views and stereotypes. In 2011, *The Book of Mormon* debuted on Broadway to critical acclaim as evidenced by numerous Tony Awards, including Best Musical, and solidified the iconic figure of the Mormon missionary for audiences. Dressed in a white button-down shirt with a black tie and dress pants, the figure of Elder Price embodies popular conceptions of Mormon missionaries – well-meaning yet misguided, naïve yet ambitious, innocent yet dangerous (see Figure 14). Having been seen by more

Figure 14 Dom Simpson playing Elder Price at West End Live in Trafalgar Square 2022. He is wearing expected LDS elder attire – black pants, a white collared shirt, and a dark tie. His hair is short, and his face is clean-shaven. Photo courtesy of Mark Davidson/Alamy Stock Photo.

than nineteen million people worldwide, *The Book of Mormon* popularizes a sympathetic, yet superficial view of Latter-Day Saints. At the same time, the musical leaves unanswered more in-depth questions about the Saints, their missionary dress codes, and the impact of stereotypes.

In the twenty-first century, opinions on Mormonism remain divided, with some still classifying it as a cult, while others view it as a mainstream religion. However, in the early years of Mormonism, which was officially established as a church in 1830, many Americans would have categorized it as a dangerous cult that threatened American democracy, the nuclear family, and Christianity itself. Accused of deception and lies on multiple levels – political, religious, and economic – opponents' attacks ranged from the rhetorical to the violent, from the literary to the physical (Corrigan & Neal 2020: 73–98). While Mormonism has gained wider acceptance over time, echoes of these historical perceptions persist in some circles today. Many of these concerns stem from the church's controversial practice of polygamy. Although never as widespread as people feared, Mormons, especially Mormon men, were stereotyped as sexually depraved, while women were depicted as enslaved by the evils of this system. This image circulated in cartoons and exposés and became a central way religious and political opponents sought to delegitimize Saints, as they were called, and their leaders, including Joseph Smith and Brigham Young. This is visualized in Figure 15 as a man, likely leader Brigham Young representing all of Mormonism, is depicted as a voracious octopus who has captured numerous innocent women beyond Salt Lake City in his far-reaching, deadly tentacles.

The startling contrast between the villainous Mormon octopus and the naïve Elder Price highlights a cultural shift in the perceptions of Saints. The Mormon image, as documented by historian Jan Shipps, began to change, and become more positive in the mid-twentieth century. During this time, the media started portraying Mormons as "neat, modest, virtuous, family-loving, conservative, and patriotic people" (2000: 100). This depiction was affirmed when *The Book of Mormon* debuted in 2011 and Mitt Romney ran for US president, a period characterized by observers and the press as a "Mormon moment" (Gordon & Shipps 2011). At the same time, despite the Church's suspension of polygamy in 1890, Romney continued to field questions and confronted widespread misconceptions that persisted in associating orthodox Mormons with the practice of polygamy, perhaps fueled in part by TV shows, including *Big Love* (2006–2011) and *Sister Wives* (2010–present).

These fissures in the Mormon moment, then, highlight the complex web of stereotypes and imagery that contemporary Saints confront, especially when going on mission. The transformation of the Mormon image from villainous to virtuous is incomplete and so provides an important context for understanding the

Figure 15 "The Mormon Octopus Enslaving the Women of Utah" from John Hanson Beadle's *Polygamy: or, The Mysteries and Crimes of Mormonism* (1870), p. xxxi. Public domain.

environment in which the Mormon missionary and their dress code works, both internally and externally. The Church strongly encourages and expects single Mormon men to go on mission for two years, typically when they reach adulthood around age 18 and 60 to 75 percent of the missionary pool is comprised of young men. Women also go on mission, but the pressure to do so is not as strong historically (ABC News 2015; Norcross 2019). Given these percentages and the historical stereotype of Mormon men, this examination focuses on the intersection of religion, dress, and gender in male missionary dress.

The "Missionary Standards for the Disciples of Jesus Christ," the handbook for aspiring LDS evangelists, frames this religious service through appeals to sacred texts, namely, the Bible (Matthew 28:19-20) and Doctrines and Covenants (59:5-6). It also emphasizes how the whole of Mormon life is a mission. It is not something "like putting on an employee or school uniform in the morning only to take it off again when the day is done." The Church reminds its representatives that mission work is a lifelong pursuit (Missionary Standards). The short-term missionary experience, including its dress codes, helps socialize and prepare Mormon youth for this spiritual expectation (Joseph 1986: 119; Stark 1987: 24–5).

Section 4.9 of the missionary handbook, which focuses on "Dress and Appearance," emphasizes its significance. "As an authorized representative of Jesus Christ and His restored Church, your appearance is often the first message others receive. Throughout your mission, make sure that your appearance and behavior help others focus on that message" (Missionary Standards). Aspiring missionaries are then sent to additional links that provide more details on the type of clothing that enhances, rather than distracts and detracts from, evangelistic work. For example, the clothing should: "fit well (not too tight or loose); not be transparent, revealing, or distracting in any way; be clean and in good repair; be free of wrinkles; be durable, easy to care for, and suitable for your mission's climate, and be easy to pack and fit in luggage" (Dress and Appearance). The linked "Guidelines for Elders" reminds readers that their attire should align with "the sacred nature of [their] calling" and provides even more detail. Expected clothing is described as "professional" and includes the following: suits (if appropriate for the mission context), dress pants, white button-down and collared shirts (now sometimes plain blue shirts are allowed), ties (not always required now), and "conservative" belts. The accompanying images show acceptable examples, and the explanatory text highlights the importance of selecting "conservative" colors and "small, simple, and subtle" patterns, as well as choosing wrinkle resistant fabrics (Guidelines for Elders; Ingram 2020). Throughout, the concept of "conservative" connotes the unremarkable, practical, and plain character of dress expected, which can be seen in Figure 16. This quasi-uniform functions to "suppress individuality" and the "individual idiosyncrasies of behavior, appearance, and sometimes physical attributes" (Joseph 1986: 68). Individuality is controlled and camouflaged, at least ideally.

These prescriptive texts emphasize the correspondence between Mormon theology and missionary dress. Not only are missionaries "representative" of the Church, but they also embody it through their behavior, speech, and clothing. His quasi-uniform attire, combined with his "conservative hairstyle" and clean-shaven face, indicates membership in the Church. More than that, though, it reflects and shapes the Church's conservative gender and sexual norms. The Church promotes "chastity," meaning that young unmarried missionaries must not have sex prior to marriage and "must be morally clean in [their] thoughts, words, and actions." Conservative attire that is not too tight, too loose, or distracting seeks to highlight the moral purity of male missionaries even as it works to discipline Mormon male bodies and minds. This dress work shapes the missionary and assures potential converts that these are authentic and sincere young men – unlike the sexually depraved caricature of the Mormon man from times past.

Wearing Their Faith 37

Figure 16 Mormon Elders wearing conservative attire, which consists of black pants, white button-down shirts, and dark, plain ties. Their hair is short, and they are clean-shaven as outlined in the dress code. Photo courtesy of Keith Morris/Alamy Stock Photo.

Dress codes, as scholar Linda Arthur reminds us, are "a visible manifestation of cultural values" (1999: 3). Ideally, this occurs at both individual and group levels. For the individual elder, distinctive attire serves as a constant reminder of the mission and purpose. The Church or group defines "what is considered normative in terms of sexuality, emotional expression and socially acceptable modes of self-presentation." Through this process of enculturation, the person internalizes these norms, behaviors, and values (Graybill & Arthur 1999: 17–18). For example, during one young man's last week of serving on mission, he had an opportunity to evangelize on his own and learned that he had successfully internalized his spiritual calling. He wrote:

> As I began to share the story of how we received the Book of Mormon, I distinctly felt in my soul that I sincerely believed every word I was saying. With a companion you teach about the Book of Mormon because you are supposed to. By myself, I could've talked about anything I wanted or say [*sic*] or nothing at all if I so pleased, but I really wanted to teach and bear testimony ... The realisation [*sic*] that I was purely acting on my own will and not for any social pressure or gain gave me an energy to teach as many

people as I could on the street that day ... purely from my own free will. (Scott 2016)

This young man's reflection demonstrates his internalization and embodiment of the missionary role. Similar to the Children of God who *became* God's endtime prophets, here we see him not only perform missionary work, but also *become* a missionary. His choice of language – sincerely, purely, freely – emphasizes this transformation and his framing of it in the language of authenticity. While he does not explicitly mention his attire, we can see in this excerpt that he has internalized its values and meanings. For the elders as a whole, the uniform qualities of their attire combined with the practice of serving in pairs or groups (and the knowledge that other elders dress and do likewise) diminish individuality, while enhancing group accountability and cohesion. As mentioned in Scott's blog, "When you do missionary work the way it should be done, with a companion, you have the pressure to contact, to teach and to testify because your companion expects you too [*sic*]" (Scott 2016). Reassurance also accompanies accountability as missionaries, as well as those in other groups, realize they are not alone. "Members of a group can identify each other and draw comfort from knowing that they are not alone when all wear the same distinctive dress" (Joseph 1986: 51). As a result, the missionary dress code helps constitute not only the missionary, but also the whole missionary community.

At the same time, the elders' distinctive dress – their quasi-uniform – is not too aberrant. Conservative colors, patterns, and styles ensure that these young men are not too flashy or strange. In addition, the quasi-uniform does not feature any explicit religious symbols and characteristics. For example, there are no physical elements that differentiate the white button-down worn by a businessperson and that worn by a Mormon elder. So, in one way the attire of Mormon missionaries is distinct and stands out, but in other ways it blends in and functions as a kind of conservative camouflage. The context in which it is worn, the youth of its wearers, and a little knowledge of Mormon missionaries make the difference. If you encounter two young men wearing this attire coming to your door or greeting you on the street, you are likely to identify them as proselytizers, rather than businessmen.

In the context of LDS evangelism, elder missionary dress helps activate what Erving Goffman calls "a moral demand." Wearing distinctive, conservative attire helps the elder look the part, define the situation, and ensure that others interpret him or her as a "person of a particular kind." In doing so, Goffman explains, the wearer "automatically exerts a moral demand upon others, obliging them to value and treat him in the manner that persons of his kind have a right to expect" (Goffman 1959: 13; Bucar 2017: 14–15). In this case, the missionary dress code helps the elder claim his status as moral, trustworthy, and sincere – someone who should be listened to, or, at least, treated with respect. At the same time, this distinctive form of dress also places a moral demand on the wearer. Observers expect certain forms of behavior and not others, when young men don this form of dress and are recognized as elders. For example, people see fire fighters and police officers in their uniforms and expect them to adhere to specific ethical and behavioral norms. Failure to do so results in public demands for accountability and justice (Joseph 1987: 50). Mormon elders face similar pressures to behave in expected ways while wearing their missionary attire. If seen drinking alcohol at a bar or swearing at a potential convert, these violations would likely result in some sort of censure, whether a call to the local LDS Church or filming the infraction and posting it on social media. In our saturated digital age, this form of accountability should not be underestimated.

The dress code for Mormon missionary men is not overt, flashy, or necessarily distinct. No symbols or designs mark this attire as specifically Mormon, but it clearly identifies to participants and outsiders alike this vocational time in a young elder's life. Unlike the overt sackcloth strategy of the Children of God that garnered media attention, the quasi-uniform of elders functions as a type of conservative camouflage that simultaneously combats prejudice, diminishes individuality, and enhances the Church's image. It reminds us that dress codes and dress work do not necessarily need to be flashy or overt. It also demonstrates how NRMs, perhaps more so than so-called mainstream religions, are continually navigating cultural expectations – past and present. In addition, this example highlights the ways NRMs and religions more broadly use dress codes and norms to socialize people, especially young people, into the values and theology of the movement. Dress work, as seen in both the Children of God and Mormonism, is a powerful way that religions can shape their members and foster authentic internalization of their beliefs and practices. At the same time, this case study, as with the previous one, illustrates that a unique dress code does not need to last a lifetime. Eighteen months to two years of abiding by the LDS missionary dress code is deemed long enough to enculturate a person into a lifetime of dressing modestly and ensuring that their sartorial choices reflect their spiritual selves.

The Nation of Islam and Dress Code Complexities

As we have seen, the Children of God used clothing to overtly confront the system and Mormon missionary attire more implicitly challenges popular conceptions and norms. An examination of the Nation of Islam's dress code, which included guidelines for both men and women, provides another example and perspective on the importance of dress and its complexity in NRMs and religious movements more broadly. While the expectations for men included suits and bowties, this analysis will focus on the dress code for women in the 1960s and early 1970s. It highlights a movement that explicitly confronted and navigated racist stereotypes through dress work. Founded in the early 1930s by W. D. Fard (c. 1877–c. 1934), the NOI taught that Christianity was a tool of the white devil "used to oppress and subjugate people of color." Fard, believed to be God incarnate, and his Prophet Elijah Muhammad (1897–1975) preached that their version of Islam was "the true and natural religion of black people." Embracing this religion would begin a process of restoring Black people's rightful and superior place in the world – creating stable families, fostering economic success, and enhancing bodily health (Reed 2016). While some scholars and critics characterize the NOI as a nationalist movement, which functions to diminish its religious dimensions, scholar of American religion Edward E. Curtis IV argues that "it is impossible to see religious and political activity within the NOI as separate categories of human behavior. To the contrary, any comprehensive understanding of the NOI should pay attention to the intersection of religious, political, social, and economic behaviors among movement members" (Curtis 2002: 186; see also Finley 2022). Thus, to study dress within the NOI fosters a greater understanding of its complex and wholistic efforts.

While scholars debate how to classify the NOI, cultural observers and opponents have long characterized it as a dangerous and problematic cult. In 1934, the *Detroit Free Press* reported that "U.S. May Fight Voodoo in City," an article that detailed a raid on the University of Islam (an NOI school) and the arrest of sixteen Black people for "contributing to the delinquency of minors." Such delinquency consisted of teaching "voodoo" practices (never defined), a substandard curriculum, and denouncing the American flag. Throughout the column, the author refers to the NOI as a "voodoo" cult, "the Cult of Islam," and simply "cult." It ends by mentioning that the movement first came into the public awareness in 1932 through a murder case "which was described as a 'human sacrifice' in keeping with the cult teachings" (see Weisenfeld 2016: 62–4). A decade later, newspapers continued to utilize cult language, emphasized the danger of the movement, and during World War II claimed that the FBI "considers it more than likely that the cult is operating under Japanese sponsorship and with Japanese aid" (*The Central New Jersey Home News* 1942).

Given its promotion of Black superiority and racial segregation, the NOI already faced heightened racial stereotypes and misconceptions. These newspaper articles amplified the perceived racialized threat embodied by the NOI by using the words "voodoo," "human sacrifice," and "Japanese sponsorship." The latter not only emphasized the potential foreign alliances that may be subverting the cause of American democracy during World War II, but also raised the specter of people of color coming together to challenge white power. Further, "voodoo" and "human sacrifice" operated, then and now, within a matrix of racialized religious otherness – representing primitive and superstitious rites practiced by uncivilized nonwhite groups. Through this language, critics sought to highlight the dangerous "African-ness" embodied by the "cult of Islam" (Weisenfeld 2016: 65).

While the NOI as a group confronted racialized characterizations of its religious practices, its Black members, both male and female, also faced pernicious racial stereotypes. Given the focus of our case study, three dominant characterizations of Black women are important to consider – the mammy, the matriarch, and the sexual siren (Hill Collins 1990: 67–90; Woodard & Mastin 2005: 266). The figure of the mammy is a loyal servant who loves and cares for white families at the expense of her own, while the matriarch conveys "the image of a controlling, emasculating Black woman who dictated to both her children and her man their place in her home" (Woodard & Mastin 2005: 271). In this regime of representational practices, Black women cannot win (Hall 1997: 261–2). The mammy neglects her own home, while the working matriarch does likewise and "is not feminine and dependent enough and hurts Black men in their traditional patriarchal role" (Woodard & Mastin 2005: 272). According to this logic, the matriarch, rather than structural racism, bears the blame "for the success or failure of Black children" (Hill Collins 1990: 74–5). The sexual siren casts Black women as "sexually aggressive, uncaring Jezebels." Crystalized during slavery, white men utilized and reinforced the sexual siren stereotype of Black women to justify sexually assaulting them (Hill Collins 1990: 77–8). In the United States, Black women, regardless of their religious affiliation, had to, and continue to, navigate these attacks on their bodies and lives. As Curtis states, "the black body has been and continues to be an important symbol of the struggle for black liberation" (Curtis 2002: 169). We can see these struggles in the NOI and its dress codes for women.

In "Islamizing the Black Body," Curtis identifies several examples of how "anxieties about the control and abuse of black bodies" appear in NOI sources, including valorizing the physical body of Muhammad Ali, the poisoning of the Black body through white foods and liquor, and the emasculation of the Black male due to "an inability to defend black women against white male sexual assault" (Curtis 2002: 170–1). We can extend Curtis's analysis to Black women and the anxieties that the NOI sought to assuage regarding their bodies, which demonstrates the movement's grappling with dominant stereotypes of Black women.

The Prophet Elijah Muhammad published a list of fifteen "evils" that NOI women had to learn through Muslim Girls Training and General Civilization Classes (MGT–GCC) – classes that women attended multiple times a week to learn about and participate in the movement. Muhammad's list emphasized the fear that improperly clad Black women would tempt and lead Black men astray. For example, item number four states, "You shall not tempt Men with your beauty in any form, by displaying nudist parts of your body. Hair, Bust, Legs, back and hips, singing love songs, enchanting looks, walking, sitting or lying down." Item number five forbids wearing "tight form fitting clothes in public," as well as prohibiting short dresses, short sleeves, and low-cut garments, for the same reason (Taylor 2017: 77). These and other items on the list highlight the NOI's fear of Black women's sexuality and power – their internalization of the Jezebel stereotype – even as they sought to debunk and fight it.

Muhammad's theology sought to challenge the stereotype as it blamed white men for luring Black women into wearing short dresses and immodest styles that degraded them. He wrote, "in order to get you to commit evil and indecency, the white man cuts your dresses off up to and above your knee" (Muhammad 1970: 16–17). Themes reinforced through columns and other materials published in *Muhammad Speaks*. For example, in June 1968, a political cartoon-like insert contained an illustrated white mother and daughter on the left. The mother wears a form-fitting, low-cut, sleeveless, above-the-knee dress. The daughter's style mimics that of her mother. The Black mother and daughter featured on the right side follow these styles. "The Filth of the Filth" captions the illustrations, and two edited scriptural verses (Matthew 26:41 and Qur'an 7:27) appear in the middle and emphasize temptation and its multiple forms – white men and women tempting Black women through their fashions, but also Black women tempting Black men through immodest dress (1968). The stereotype of Black woman as temptress persisted within the movement given, as scholars of the NOI acknowledge, its conservative gender ideology (Gibson & Karim 2014: 40–2).

The solution to these anxieties was twofold. First, it included modest dress and eventually an official dress code for MGT–GCC classes; and second, it urged female followers to embrace their "natural beauty." Modest dress expectations and practices, meaning long skirts, long sleeves, high-necked bodices, and head coverings had a long history in the movement. Muhammad's wife Clara regularly dressed in longer skirts, long-sleeved and high-necked blouses, and wore a scarf as a head covering. She created the de facto uniform of the movement (see Figure 17), which was then revised by her daughter Ethel Muhammad Sharrieff in 1967 when the dress code was made mandatory (Wheeler 2021, 2023). NOI women embraced the dress code, which was

Figure 17 Nation of Islam women wearing their white uniforms and headcoverings to a religious convention in New York City in 1963. Photo courtesy of Everett Collection Historical/Alamy Stock Photo.

highlighted at religious gatherings and in photographs of female NOI members published in *Muhammad Speaks*. Modest dress transformed Black women from "tempting" to "respectable," from "indecent" to "civilized" (Muhammad 1970). It highlighted their acquisition of self-knowledge – learning about the movement's view of their authentic and esteemed heritage as part of a superior group and their place as "mothers of civilization" (King 2017: 220–4; Wheeler 2023). It also visualized the alignment between their spiritual and sartorial selves. In this way, the dress code provided a solution to the supposed problem posed by Black women's bodies within the movement and without.

The modestly dressed female NOI member no longer tempted Black men and, at the same time, developed respect for herself and demanded it from others, Black and white. After contrasting her modest dress with that of her tight pant-wearing classmates, Sister Sylvia D. X wrote, "I saw something which they could not understand or see, … Among these things were respect for myself" (1967: 25). Sister Fatima X connected modest dress with specific behaviors and respect. "Their manners are perfect. They are cultured and quiet; they personify all that the word lady implies. These women are real ladies, and due the respect of civilized people all over the world" (1967: 25). Dress work was transformative and powerful. Similarly, Sister Alease X emphasized her obedience to the dress code and its resulting rewards. "Everywhere I go, each and every day, I dress the way the Messenger has taught me, my clothes down to my ankle. I get the highest respect from black and white because of this" (1967: 25). Sister Shirley Moton described it this way: "I wear the clothes of a civilized people. My dresses are far below my knees and I love it. This makes me respect myself better but it also makes other people respect me" (1966: 25). The dress code, as Goffman argues, exerted a "moral demand" on the wearers and their behavior, as well as on how those within the community, and at times on those without, treated female NOI members (Goffman 1959: 13).

Muhammad also encouraged Black women in the movement to reject the dominant white beauty standards and to reclaim their authentic heritage and natural beauty. In his list of rules sent to women of the NOI, Muhammad urged Black women to reject makeup, and "hot irons," and bleaching creams. He insisted, "you are Natural beautiful without make ups [*sic*]" (Taylor 2017: 77). Sister Shirley Moton moved seamlessly from her discussion of the dress code to that of beauty. "The Honorable Elijah Muhammad teaches us that we, black women here in America, are the most beautiful of all women. We have our own natural beauty and we do not have to be made up by using white women's makeup" (1967: 25). Mrs. Margaret J. X. wrote, "I am proud to have been among the most beautiful women in the wilderness of North America – the Muslim women" before discussing modest dress. After emphasizing how Christian styles "change every year," she highlights how "Muslim men and women ... outstanding in their uniforms, suits or dresses, show nothing but original beauty" (1967: 25). This claiming of natural or original beauty allowed NOI women to proudly proclaim, "I know that I am a mother of civilization" (Moton 1966). It reinforced the idea that Black women could reject dominant stereotypes and reclaim their authentic and esteemed selves (see Figure 18).

Theologically, the prescribed attire also worked to align the NOI with the global Islamic community, creating tangible, visible connections between women in the US and Muslim women in other countries. For example, an article entitled "Indecency in Female Dress Still Not Tolerated in Islam," outlined the expected dress practices for Muslim women in Egypt, which highlighted their similarity with NOI dress norms (Muhammad Speaks 1967; Sharrieff 1968). On one level this bolstered the Nation's claims to Islamic legitimacy and authenticity; however, it also provided fuel for opponents who sought to characterize the group as a "cult" and viewed their dress code as "foreign" and "un-American" (Curtis 2002: 183; Taylor 2017: 68).

While some NOI women, especially those published in *Muhammad Speaks*, extolled the benefits of modest dress, the reality on the ground was more complex.

Figure 18 Close-up photograph of a young woman at the 1972 Savior's Day service in her MGT attire. Photo courtesy of Robert Abbott Sengstacke/Getty Images.

In their in-depth study, *Women of the Nation*, Gibson and Karim note that NOI women who worked outside the group were immediately identifiable because of their distinct dress and often endured discrimination, rather than garnering respect (2014: 68). And in *The Promise of Patriarchy*, Taylor recounts the story of Sister Gwendolyn 2X who never wore the uniform while at work outside the NOI, as well as accounts of other women not wearing the headscarf at their jobs, whether employed by the NOI or not (2017: 115). In addition, at least some NOI women chafed at the dress requirements, prompting Elijah Muhammad to issue a "Warning to M.G.T. and G.C. Class" in 1968. In this text, he prohibited NOI women from "adopting the African dress and hair styles" and forbade "accepting traditional African tribal styles and garments with gay colors." Those who violated the dress code would be dismissed (Muhammad 1968). Others sought to create flexibility within the confines of the dress code. M.G.T. classes would hold fashion shows that demonstrated ways to "accessorize" and personalize their modest apparel (Gibson & Karim 2014: 51). These instances show the nuances and layers of dress work. It highlights the ways NOI women customized the dress code to their needs on a situational basis – sometimes wearing the whole uniform, sometimes wearing parts of it, and sometimes accessorizing it. Rather than conceptualizing NRM dress codes as rigid, zero-sum structures that demand complete obedience, these examples show how women negotiated the dress code and made it work for them.

Through this case study, we can see the complexities of the NOI's dress code for its female members in the late 1960s and early 1970s. It highlights the complex circularity of power that characterizes representational practices (Hall 1997: 261–2). The NOI insistence on a modest dress code for women reflects, in part, its internalization of stereotypes and its simultaneous commitment to fighting them. It is important though, as Curtis argues, to understand these processes as being "connected to, rather than determined by," the racialized contexts in which the NOI existed (Curtis 2002: 176). This approach highlights the powerful ways structural racism constrains people and groups, but also how people create space and claim power within and despite those barriers. Recognizing this complexity highlights the significance of NOI dress work in the formation of faithful followers loyal to the movement. Many Black women in the NOI found modest dress and natural beauty to be powerful tools of spiritual transformation – fostering self-respect and self-knowledge. More than that, though, it provided Black women with a tangible way to combat pernicious racialized stereotypes and cultivate their authentic identities as "mothers of civilization."

Conclusion

The hegemonic cult stereotype utilizes ideas about dress codes and uniformity to portray those who join these movements as gullible, brainwashed victims – people who have lost their individuality and sense of self. These three case studies of dress in NRMs demonstrate not only the misleading character of this conceptualization, but also the complex and varied role that dress work plays in the creation and maintenance of NRMs and religions more broadly. These examples also highlight that many members of these groups, contrary to the superficial understandings, do not experience dress work as oppressive. Rather, most find it to be a religious practice that strengthens their spirituality and enlivens their commitment to the religion. As David Morgan writes, "Belief should not be understood as coming only before such things as the veneration of relics or the ecstatic drudgery of pilgrimage, but as being constituted by them. People do what they want to believe. They make belief in the things they do" (Morgan 2010: 11–12). Put another way, belief does not, or does not only, precede dress work, but the dress work that people perform constitutes a vital way that belief happens. It is how members of these groups become endtime prophets, missionaries, and mothers of civilization. These become identities that they find religiously meaningful and frame as authentic reflections of their embodied lives. While authenticity is a complex, constructed category (Grazian 2010), clothing functions as a vital way for members of these groups to confront and challenge societal stereotypes and lay claim to who they think they really are at a given moment in time. As a result, rather than stereotypes associating clothing with artifice or simplistic associations of dress codes with unthinking uniformity, we can see the power and variety of dress work in these three

NRMs. Religiously inspired dress practices are short-term and long-term, impact men and women, enhance individual commitment, and strengthen group cohesion. Complex and varied, these dress practices and those of other NRMs, such as ISKCON (Zeller 2023), the UNIA (McCormick 2008), the Raelians (Palmer & Gareau 2017), Heaven's Gate (Corrigan & Neal 2020), and others, show us the power of clothing in religious life. And in the next section, we examine the complex intersection of the cult stereotype, NRMs, and the fashion industry.

3 Fashion and the Maintenance of the Cult Stereotype

Fashion and religion have a long-entwined history. Given the dominance of Western cities and designers in the fashion industry, Christianity has functioned as its de facto religion and can be seen infusing its language, advertising, and designs. Since the mid-twentieth century, designs inspired by Christian figures (monks, nuns, priests), as well as garments featuring Christian symbols (Mary, Jesus, saints, the cross) have become increasingly common on fashion runways. Other religions have occasionally appeared, including Judaism, Hinduism, and Islam, often causing controversy and evoking debates about appropriation (Neal 2019). Whether met with acclaim or criticism, fashion designers find in religions a repository of symbols and artifacts that they employ in the name of beauty, art, and inspiration. NRMs, however, have rarely been utilized or identified as a source of fashion.

In 2018 this changed. Two forms of dress worn by groups labeled cults – the prairie dresses of the Fundamentalist Church of Jesus Christ of Latter-Day Saints (FLDS) and the red hues of the Rajneeshees – appeared prominently on the fashion radar. By examining these two case studies, we can see the complicated relationship between NRMs, fashion, and the cult stereotype. These case studies demonstrate how this biased framing works within the context of fashion. As with other cultural forms, fashion fosters a particular vision of what constitutes good, or at least better, religion and we can see this in an examination of 2018's cult-inspired fashions. At that time, fashion critics and followers celebrated the red worn by the Rajneeshees and cited it as a source of fashion invention, while the FLDS went unmentioned amid the popularity of prairie dresses. The exoticism and sexual liberation associated with the Rajneeshees made it a seemingly better cult and thus a more creative fashion source, in contrast to the rigidity of a fundamentalist sect of the Mormon branch of Christianity. However, while the Rajneeshees were deemed more fashionable than the FLDS, both groups continued to be framed and understood through this stereotypical lens.

This negative perception, which equates deviant dress with dangerous theology, typically means that these groups are deemed too problematic to stimulate fashion. The general lack of in-depth knowledge about NRMs amplifies the stereotype and makes their omission from fashion even more understandable. Further, historically, religious movements with distinct forms of dress often explicitly reject the garments and ethos of the fashion industry and frame their clothing in opposition to fashion. Some scholars have defined this action and these garments as "antifashion"; however, scholars Susan B. Kaiser and Ryan Looysen (2010) point out that "remaining outside of fashion actually requires a keen awareness of fashion. How else is one to know that they are wearing antifashion as opposed to fashion?" Rather than antifashion, Kaiser and Looysen argue for the term "oppositional dress" meaning "the dissent or distinctive ideas of a group, or views hostile to the conformist majority," as defined by sociologist of fashion Elizabeth Wilson. This conceptualization avoids oversimplistic binaries such as fashion/anti-fashion and reification of categories.

Oppositional dress is often espoused by countercultural and subcultural movements, Hippies, Beats, and bikers are just a few examples. However, even as groups such as these utilize dress to critique fashion and elements of the dominant culture, "the dominant culture relies upon oppositional dress of all kinds for inspiration and marketing" (Kaiser & Looysen 2010). The biker jacket of the streets becomes the business casual moto jacket of the office. In this way, once-oppositional trends are incorporated and made part of the fashion mainstream. For example, in terms of religion, the plain dress of the Amish (see Figure 19) and the oppositional styles of Catholic monks, nuns, and priests have often been mined as sources of inspiration by fashion designers ranging from Geoffrey Beene to Jean Paul Gaultier, from Calvin Klein to Michael Kors (Neal 2019: 119–53). However, while a few may categorize the Amish and Catholic Christianity as cults, most would not, so the incorporation of their styles and symbols into fashion may shock or delight but they do so without raising the specter of the cult stereotype. This was not the case when the public encountered FLDS fashion in the spring of 2008.

Prairie Dresses: From Mockery to Modest Fashion

In 2008, a phone call to police alleged that children were being physically and sexually abused at the Yearning for Zion Ranch, an FLDS community in Eldorado, Texas. This prompted a law enforcement raid on the community, resulting in the evacuation and eventual separation of the women and children in

Figure 19 A large group of Amish women and a few Amish men walking along a street in Gordonville, Pennsylvania in 2011. The Amish women wear long pastel dresses with dark tights, bonnets to cover their hair, and winter jackets. Photo courtesy of Planetpix/Alamy Stock Photo.

the community. Extensive investigations led to some FLDS men being convicted of first- and second-degree sexual assault of a child; however, the Texas Third Court of Appeals ruled that the state had "insufficient grounds for the 'extreme' measure" of separating mothers and their children and they were eventually reunited (ACLU 2008). While not the only Mormon sect that practices polygamy, the FLDS emerged as one of the most prominent through media coverage of the raid. The dresses and hairstyles worn by women in the movement made it even more sensational and within days prompted extended fashion commentary. Headlines proclaimed: "The Flamboyance of Simplicity," "Polygamists Make their Own Fashion Statement," and "Latter-Day Restraints" (Givhan 2008; Lo 2008; NBC News 2008). The oppositional dress donned by FLDS women, as seen in Figure 20, presented fashion critics and media observers with sartorial choices that demanded explanation.

The media coverage initially expressed a kind of enlightened, yet puzzled, disdain of FLDS women's style before moving into more sustained critique. One writer asked, "Do we have to call it polygamy chic?" (Wilson 2008), while another, writing for the *New York Post*, explained: "Puffy polyester dresses, sporty Skechers sneakers, sky-high bangs (circa the late '80s) and a unibrow

Figure 20 Two FLDS women and their daughters photographed in 2008. They wear pastel prairie dresses with long sleeves, high necklines, and below the knee skirts. Photo courtesy of UPI/Alamy Stock Photo.

might just be your ticket to heaven. Who knew?" (Lo 2008). Sarcasm and witticisms abounded in the coverage, and some simply derided it. NBC News, for instance, consulted "celebrity stylist and salon owner Ted Gibson" for comment. After labeling the attire "homely," Gibson goes on to interpret the dress and style: "It says, 'I don't care very much. I really don't have time to worry about the way that I look, because I have 20 children'" (2008). Gibson's lack of expertise regarding the FLDS aside, his condemnation is clear.

In the media coverage, FLDS women's dress and hairstyles provided evidence of their exploitation and lack of choice within the movement. The seeming sameness (at least to outsiders) of the long prairie dresses with high collars, puffed sleeves, and pastel colors functioned as visible proof that individual personal autonomy had been restricted to an alarming degree. For example, when interviewing young women in the community in 2009, Oprah asked, "why all the dresses looked alike. The girls affirmed that they covered their bodies because the body was sacred. One girl explained that the dresses are unique, but don't seem different to outsiders. Oprah chuckled and replied, 'Olive, that is funny!'" (Baker). Oprah's laughter placed her and the viewers in the position of enlightened interpreters who knew more than Olive, and by extension other FLDS women. Emphasizing cult conformity, the media largely ignored the intricate stitching and patterning details that women in the community utilized to create their own sense of individual style. For outsiders, dressing the same, meant thinking the same, which indicated brainwashing and cult control over FLDS members. In addition, instead of seeing the women's complicated hairstyles – elaborate braids, sausage curls, and rolled hair (often without the aid of a curling iron) – as evidence of individuality and fashion, the media framed it as another form of exploitation (see Figure 21). According to one article, "To an outside observer, their hairstyle speaks of control, dignity, reserve and, of course, femininity – the kind that is carried as a burden, rather than admired" (Givhan 2008). The article seems to be asking: Why would women spend this much time on these outdated hairstyles? As if spending time on beauty routines is an abnormal thing to do. The article never provides an insider perspective to complicate that of the "outside observer," and implies that other forms of fashion and the pressure of American beauty standards are not burdensome.

Such questions and criticisms were often followed by comparing the dresses to prison apparel. Writing for the *Washington Post* fashion editor Robin Givhan explained, "They look as though they are dressed in the washed-out hues of institutional garb, a bit like old-fashioned prison inmates" (2008), and another stated, "The compound isn't the only cage for the women of polygamy. There is also a prison uniform – yards of pink and blue fabric, and inches and inches of hair and ugly orthopedic shoes" (Lo 2008; Walsh 2008). Interviews with former FLDS members, such as Carolyn Jessop, amplified this imprisonment

Figure 21 A 2008 photograph of FLDS women with their elaborately styled hair. Each wears a slightly different hairstyle. Also apparent is the variety in the color and details of their prairie dresses. Photo courtesy of Bob Daemmrich/ Alamy Stock Photo.

interpretation. In a segment with CBS, she highlighted not only the abuse she suffered as a plural wife, but also the limitations and restrictions women face in their dress and in their lives (CBS News 2008). The coverage does not use the word "cult"; however, its deployment of prison language and metaphors identify its cult lens. In his discussion of NRMs, scholar of religion David Chidester explains that in "modern, industrialized, western societies ... there have been two major categories for imagining otherness: the prison and the asylum." He continues,

> As alternative worldviews, alternative ethical orientations, and alternative political orders, marginal religious groups necessarily stand on the boundary of the larger society. Consistently they have been depicted in newspapers, electronic media, and popular psychologizing in precisely this vocabulary of exteriority. Marginal religious movements surface within this imagination of otherness clothed in the dominant metaphoric images generated by the prison and the asylum. (1988: 24–7)

Thus, even without explicitly labeling the FLDS a cult, the language and content used in these articles frames it in terms of the hegemonic stereotype, including, but not limited to, violations of personal autonomy, the oppression of women, and rituals of sexual deviancy. Further, the media's failure to mention any other religions – Christianity, Islam, Judaism, for example – or religious roles – priests, monks, nuns – that encourage distinct styles of dress or those that value modesty amplified the seeming strangeness of FLDS women's attire and established its cult status. "Bad fashion signals bad religion," as Kelly Baker persuasively argues in her article "Fashionable Intolerance." She explains that "by attacking polygamist chic" the media fueled this negative cult conception without directly questioning the religion of the FLDS itself (Baker).

Media coverage also expressed fears that the bad fashion exhibited by FLDS women would be contagious. As early as April 21, less than three weeks after the raid, one article included a section entitled "Influencing This Season's Fashions?" that noted the returning popularity of pastel colors and long hair (NBC News 2008). These concerns increased when FLDS women created a website, FLDSDress.com (now defunct) to sell some of their children's clothing styles. *Salon* reported that the money raised would "help women to pay for apartments they've been renting since the raid," but at the same time, asked "who's going to buy clothing associated with a polygamous sect that may well be perpetuating child rape?" (Berman 2008). Eric Wilson, reporting for the *New York Times*, expressed surprise at the venture and at the "variety of children's styles" available to purchase. These same media outlets and others, though, fearfully wondered if the fashion industry, which voraciously seeks its innovation in history, religion, and other places, would find it in FLDS dress. Wilson concluded his article with the following:

> Designers have been tempted to mine cultures with an insensitive and not entirely comprehending eye in the past. For example, Donna Karan and Yves Saint Laurent have borrowed liberally from peoples Aboriginal to Maasai, and Jean Paul Gaultier once based a men's wear collection on traditional Hasidic attire. The Easter egg palette and box-pleat, huge princess-sleeve styles of the polygamist wives may still prove irresistible. But who does their hair? (Wilson 2008)

Ultimately, though, fashion observers concluded that FLDS dress and style would not impact the mainstream fashion industry. Some joked that maybe it would function as a Halloween costume or could see "the Brooklyn hipsters rocking a French braid, but not in a serious way. Maybe ironically" (NBC News 2008). And fashion critics, like the fashion cycle, moved on.

That is until 2018, a decade after the raid on the Yearning for Zion Ranch, when prairie dresses became one of the on-trend fashion staples. Hints of a fashion shift emerged in the preceding years as styles began moving toward longer skirts, higher necklines, and flowy silhouettes (Friedman 2017). For example, in 2015, Véronique Hyland (now *Elle*'s Fashion Features Director) wrote an article for *The Cut* entitled "Introducing Cultcore: A Caftan for Every Day of the Week." The article consists of different looks from New York Fashion Week that Hyland deemed to be cult-like. The brief textual introduction defines cult style as "drapey caftans, standard-issue jumpsuits, and vacant expressions" on models' faces. The fashion photographs are accompanied by captions that include the name of the designer and some seemingly witty but derogatory reference to cults or cult-like behavior, such as "Loose silhouettes please our intergalactic overlords," "Where else do people wear identical floor-length T-shirt dresses?" and "She who wears the golden orb must be obeyed." The curated looks are loose-fitting, long – whether sleeves, pants, or dresses – and mostly monochromatic. Prints are rare, such as a very sedate pinstripe, and adornment is minimal. Hyland's introduction, captions, and the looks selected for the slideshow emphasize homogeneous dressing, fanatical obedience, and excessive modesty (2015). There is no mention of changing fashion trends, accepted religions that dress differently, or the designers' inspirations. Nor do past trends such as ascetic dressing, religious-inspired styles, or FLDS prairie dresses appear. Rather, the article provides visual fuel that reflects and fosters a stereotypical view of cults.

Then, in November 2018, *Elle (Australia)* published an article entitled "Dressing like You're In a Cult Is Next Season's Most Covetable Fashion Trend" (Chowdury

2018). It begins: "If you feel like your new-season wardrobe is heading further and further towards 'cult' territory – think floor-grazing dresses, high ruffled necklines, and that particular brand of unobtrusive patterning – you're not alone. Cults (yes, like the Mansons, like the Source Family, like the Rajneeshpuram commune) are certainly having a moment in the cultural zeitgeist right now." The article goes on to chronicle upcoming films about Charles Manson, the cult theme in the current season of *American Horror Story*, and the docuseries streaming, including *Wild Wild Country* and *Waco*. Notably, the FLDS are not mentioned. The attention then shifts back to the "alarmingly beguiling" trend, which again emphasizes the features of this style – "high necklines, full-length sleeves, ankle-grazing hemlines, ruffles, prairie-style dresses, and a strange tendency towards 'safety in numbers' (the trend is best donned in groups)" (Chowdury 2018). The only potential nod to context or the past is a brief mention that the trend is influenced by "modest fashion," no further information is supplied. The article does note that "cults and fashion have long had a symbiotic relationship" and explains that fashion has been a way to signal one's belonging to a group. However, lest readers become too sympathetic to cults, the author quickly cites reasons for distancing oneself from them. The role of fashion in the Manson trial is described, and the article also explains how Nike officially discontinued its Decade sneakers – the shoes that were worn by members of Heaven's Gate when they committed suicide (or as members understood it, as they transitioned to the Next Level). The article further distances the fashion trend from so-called cult-dress and behavior by noting that "High collars are mitigated by sheer bodices. Prairie dresses are toughened up with combat boots." Such self-awareness in donning and styling this attire is necessary to reclaim it from its cult roots (Chowdury 2018).

The clothing featured in this article resembles that highlighted in the article on cultcore. Many of the outfits are monochromatic, feature long sleeves, and long, full skirts. Some of the prairie dresses, though, are made of floral fabrics, rather than the solid pastels of the FLDS. Nowhere are the FLDS or the events of 2008 mentioned. Strikingly, fashion editor for the *Washington Post* Robin Givhan, who reported on FLDS fashion and prairie dresses in 2008, does not mention the FLDS at all in her 2018 article entitled "Prairie Dresses – Yes, Prairie Dresses – Are the Most Provocative Thing in Fashion Right Now." The article chronicles the rise of designer Batsheva Hay, "who has a love of prairie dresses and buttoned-up ruffly blouses in old-fashioned cotton." Givhan, the same writer who ten years earlier compared pastel prairie dresses to prison garb, now urged readers to "not pooh-pooh prairie dresses," as Hay's designs are "modest," "pure," and "earnest." Her use of contemporary fabrics combined with the prairie dress style produces, according to Givhan, "a visually symbolic rejection of the slickness of contemporary life." Perhaps implicitly it is also a rejection of cult

Figure 22 Actress Ginnifer Goodwin wearing a prairie dress designed by Batsheva Hay in December 2018. Photo courtesy of Donato Sardella/Getty Images for Tamara Mellon.

life, as Givhan assures readers that "Batsheva eschews anonymity. There's no hiding in these clothes" (2018b).

Designer Batsheva Hay is the darling of these articles, as Givhan and others frequently highlight her and her work (see Figure 22). Hay's occupational pedigree (she was a lawyer), her New York roots (Queens and "not some windswept Nebraska prairie"), and her love of vintage Laura Ashley distance her from any potential rural or cult associations (Givhan 2018a). Another article mentions that Hay "explored imagery of Amish women whose plain clothing is often seen as an expression of compliance with their accepted order," and while the Amish have long been romanticized in American culture – unlike groups deemed cults – the article is quick to distance Hay and her designs from obedience and acceptance. Hay's clothes, the article assures readers, "are not about blending in – they're often too dramatic or wacky to be wallflower-y," and later Hay describes how she "hated wearing suits" and revels in her feminine creations (Farrell 2019).

In addition to her love of vintage Laura Ashley, Hay's interest in more modest designs stems from her husband's conversion to Orthodox Judaism. Mentions of her religious background, though, highlight her upbringing in a secular Jewish family and note that it was her husband who converted. Rather than being described as a convert like her husband, articles talk about Hay as "running an Orthodox household." One article even goes to great lengths to assure readers that Orthodox Judaism is not one monolithic tradition. The article then highlights how Hay carefully navigates and negotiates Orthodoxy – observing Shabbat dinner, making kosher wine, but not covering her hair (Russell 2018; Wolfson 2018). Such attention to Hay's religious life assures readers that she is no cult member or rigid conservative; rather, she is a sophisticated, creative, and thoughtful urban dweller inspired by the earnest devotion she sees in her husband, the Orthodox Jewish community of New York, and apparently the Amish.

A few of the 2018 articles, notably the feature story in *Elle (Australia)*, chronicling the rise of prairie dresses mention the word "cult" or the idea of cults; however, none that I found in my research specifically cite the FLDS and the fashion furor that surrounded the Eldorado raid in 2008. It is as if this fascination with FLDS apparel in 2008 had not happened. Yet, we know, in addition to this coverage, that the styles of 2008 and 2018 share many similar features – necklines, hemlines, long sleeves. Further, after 2008, the prairie-dress style became part of the visual stereotype of the FLDS through popular media. For example, the *Criminal Minds* episode entitled "Minimal Loss" blended elements of the events at Jonestown, Waco, and Eldorado. Airing six months after the raid, the episode featured men wearing flannel shirts and women wearing longer skirts and floral printed dresses (in stark contrast to the business attire worn by the BAU agents) and recalled images of Eldorado (2008). And in 2015, the pilot episode of *The Unbreakable Kimmy Schmidt* depicted the series protagonist and the three other wives wearing pastel prairie dresses and sporting long, carefully styled hair, as they emerged from their kidnapping by Doomsday cultist Reverend Richard Wayne Gary Wayne (see Figure 23).

While we cannot definitively conclude whether the FLDS women's dress had a direct impact on the 2018 prairie dress trend, we do know that its absence from 2018 coverage of it is significant. Fashion is a referential industry. Designers draw inspiration from art and nature, history and religion. They utilize these sources to tell stories through their collections and draw in audiences. Enlivening and re-envisioning these referents become part of the genius and acclaim attributed to fashion designers. Perhaps designers did not find the prairie dresses of the FLDS to be a fitting muse, but it seems as likely, or even

Figure 23 Still photo from *The Unbreakable Kimmy Schmidt* that shows her and the other wives wearing pastel prairie dresses and long, styled hair. Photo courtesy of Album/Alamy Stock Photo.

more likely, that the FLDS were not deemed to be an appropriate source of fashion stimulation and thus could not be explicitly named. The popular association of FLDS prairie dresses with fundamentalist forms of Christianity and the physical and sexual subjugation of women justified in the name of religion seemingly present too big an obstacle for designers to overcome and buyers to accept. Fashion designers and items can have cult followings, fashion critics can identify cult-like attire, but direct inspiration from groups deemed to be cults seems, at least in this instance, unacceptable.

As or more important, though, are the contrasting ways that the fashion industry judged FLDS women in 2008 and those embracing the 2018 prairie dress trend. In 2008, the fashion industry characterized FLDS women's attire as ugly and lacking in individuality – a kind of cult prison uniform. In contrast, in 2018, the trend is described positively as earnest, thoughtful, and modest. The biggest difference, it seems, is not the clothing, but the bodies wearing it and their given contexts. Here we vividly see the arbitrariness of the cult stereotype. What is criticized cult attire one day can become celebrated chic or subcultural style the next. The media coverage framed FLDS women's wearing of prairie dresses as inauthentic, rather than viewing their attire as an expression of FLDS women's devotion to their faith and commitment to modesty. It was interpreted as something forced upon them and thus could not authentically express their *real* identity. In contrast, women like Batsheva Hay and her celebrity clients (Ginnifer Goodwin, Naomi Watts, Maude Apatow, Christina Ricci, Beanie Feldstein, and others) are portrayed as autonomous subjects freely making the choice to wear prairie dresses (see Figure 24). Hay and those who buy her garments could wear anything and they are selecting these modest styles. As a result, the prairie dress and their carefully curated styles must accurately reflect who they really are. Thus, women outside the bounds of so-called cults become the exemplars for how to be authentically modest.

This dynamic is not new or unique to this context. For example, scholars have documented how Indian and Middle Eastern women are encouraged to stop wearing henna if they want to become modern and successful. As a result, traditions are lost; but then white Western women come in to learn about, study, and wear henna and are seen as enlightened saviors of this tradition. As Sunaina Maira argues, "The 'recovery' of henna by U.S. entrepreneurs is tied to their

Figure 24 Prairie dress featuring a bold blue and red print with white ruffle and neckerchief designed by Batsheva Hay for her Fall/Winter Ready-to-Wear Collection 2019–2020. Note the model's elaborately braided and curled hair. Photo courtesy of Victor Virgile/Getty Images.

implicit critique of Third World societies where women are both too modernized to know their own rituals but also too repressed, or even oppressed, to fully enjoy their potential sensuality" (2002: 140; Durham 2001).

Similarly, prior to our current, more open debates about cultural appropriation, when Western white women would wear the dress of another culture, such as saris or garments featuring Navajo designs, they would be seen as enlightened, cosmopolitan, or hip (see Figure 25), while women from those cultures wearing the same designs would be seen "as 'traditional,' at best 'exotic,' and certainly always 'other'" (Maira 2002: 140). We can see a similar dynamic at work in the case of the prairie dress as what was once mocked becomes an esteemed symbol of authentic modesty, fashionable rebellion, and maybe even proper faith – if worn by those who exhibit the right sort of religion. Whether deemed culturally acceptable or not, fashion has long extracted inspiration from various eras, movements, and figures. In doing so, it has cultivated a sophisticated and proper

Figure 25 Actress Helen Mirren wearing an Indian silk sari to the Emmy Awards in 2004. Photo courtesy of Featureflash Archive/Alamy Stock Photo.

way of seeing religion (Neal 2019), which maintains the cult stereotype and fosters dominant views of what religion is and should be.

Fashion's 2018 embrace of the prairie dress after its mockery of it a decade earlier highlights both the enduring power of the cult stereotype and its arbitrariness. Fashion critics utilize this framing to identify cultcore trends and styles, which then serve to reinforce it. The stereotype functions as both hermeneutic and evidence. Further, when fashion followers, rather than cult members, wear these garments they are seen as stylish, on-trend, and expressing their authentic selves, rather than as backward, unfashionable, and oppressed. An FLDS woman is no Batsheva Hay. In this case, we can see the complex ways that fashion simultaneously incorporates cult styles even as it works to maintain and police the boundaries around what constitutes good religion.

Rajneeshee Red: From Forgotten Cult to Fashion Fad

At the same time that prairie dresses surged in popularity, the docuseries *Wild Wild Country* (2018) debuted on Netflix and captured audience attention. Many had not heard of Bhagwan Shree Rajneesh (1931–1990; later known as Osho), his movement's settlement in Oregon, or the tumultuous events that followed. Rajneesh began his work as a religious teacher in the 1960s and then established the Shree Rajneesh Ashram in Pune, India, in the 1970s. His teachings blended elements of Hinduism, Buddhism, and "personal-growth philosophy," with an acceptance of materiality and sexuality. For Rajneesh, "the ideal human is Zorba the Buddha, a consummate being combining Buddha's spiritual focus with Zorba's life-embracing traits" (Goldman 2005). In 1981, Rajneesh and thousands of his followers moved to a rural community in Oregon and began building their own settlement, called Rajneeshpuram (Urban 2015). Conflicts with the surrounding townspeople escalated over time, which culminated in the infamous salad bar poisonings, attempted assassinations, and the eventual demise of the community. While these events grabbed headlines, eventually the movement faded from scrutiny and memory. That is, until filmmakers Chapman Way and Maclain Way, known at the time for *The Battered Bastards of Baseball* (2014), were approached by the film archivist of the Oregon Historical Society, who informed them that the society had "300 hours of archive footage about . . . 'the most bizarre story that ever happened in the history of Oregon.'" Four years later, *Wild Wild Country* aired (Michel 2018; Sandberg 2018).

Viewers found this oft-overlooked movement remarkable and shocking, but even more they expressed fascination for the clothes. Two tweets included in *Elle*'s "Dressing Like You're In a Cult Is Next Season's Most Covetable

Fashion Trend" captured this interest. One stated, "Anyone watching@wild-wildcountry? Just finished the first two. Imagine hundreds of people in orange turning up in your town one day" and another "Just started watching Wild Wild Country on Netflix ... I keep vacillating between 'what the hell is wrong with these people?' and 'I would totally wear that outfit'" (Chowdury 2018). Other tweets echoed this enchantment: "I honestly rlly [sic] like the Rajneesh monochrome outfit situations they had going on," "I'm watching wild wild country like uhhhh thought this was suppose [sic] to be about a cult not a dope new way of living with sick outfits. Where do I sign up?" and "Wild Wild Country is great and is also a love note to how timeless tonal blocking outfits looks [sic]" (Slone 2018). In her article entitled "Why Are People So Obsessed with This 1980s Cult's Style?" fashion critic Isabel Slone concludes that the movement's "tequila sunrise-inspired style" appears "inimitably fresh," as it highlights the "eternal timelessness of monochromic looks" and provides a colorful respite from fashion's prolonged "goth phase" (Slone 2018). The article concludes with photographs and links to numerous red items that readers can purchase. Similarly, after providing a brief synopsis of the Rajneesh movement as told by the docuseries, the article "An Entire Wardrobe Inspired by the Rajneeshee Movement of 'Wild Wild Country'" quickly turns to fashion that resembles the "remarkable all-red ensembles" worn by members. Readers are guided by photographs to stylish red dresses, as well as red tops and pants (Karefa-Johnson 2018). Other articles and posts, such as *Architectural Digest's* "We're So into the *Wild Wild Country* Color Scheme and We're Not Sorry" and "Shopping with a Client Inspired by the Colors from the Documentary Wild Wild Country," follow a similar format – a brief overview of the movement filtered through the lens of the docuseries followed by long lists of photographs and links to a range of red-hued home décor and fashion items to purchase (Raes 2018; Sims 2018). As one author explained, "Just because it's a cult doesn't mean it can't also be design inspo" (Sims 2018).

Unlike the FLDS and the prairie dress, Rajneesh and his followers are explicitly named and identified as fashion and design inspiration-worthy. Given that both groups have been labeled cults in the popular imagination, what accounts for this different treatment? To answer this question, we need to look at how the Rajneesh dress code differs from that of the FLDS and other NRMs examined in Section 2. The dress codes of the LDS, NOI, and FLDS focus on wearing specific garments with attributes that meet the community's standards of modesty, as well as their ideas about gender and sexuality – whether that is a white dress shirt and navy-blue pants or the MGT-GCC uniform. In contrast, the Rajneesh dress code is focused on color, rather than specific types of garments or hemlines and sleeve lengths (see Figure 26). As

Figure 26 Devotees wearing different kinds of clothes in varying shades of red come out to see Osho-Rajneesh drive by in his Rolls Royce at Rajneeshpuram in 1982. Photo courtesy of Rob Crandall/Alamy Stock Photo.

numerous articles reported in the wake of *Wild Wild Country*, followers of Rajneesh "wore clothes 'of the colors of the rising or setting sun' – red, orange, or purple – as well as beaded necklaces with a locket containing a picture of Bhagwan's face" (Petrarca 2018a). Others cited an interview with Ma Preem Veena from the *Statesman Journal* (Salem, Oregon), who recounted its inspiration.

> One day, Bhagwan was deciding what color his sannyasin (disciples) should wear. He looked out a window and saw the green of a tree and thought that would be a good color and represent new growth. He looked higher in the tree and saw it was a flame tree, with a big umbrella of red and gold and orange flowers. Bhagwan said, "I saw the red was flaming. I want my disciples to be the flaming of their human potential." (*Statesman Journal* 1983; *LA Times* 1985; Chua 2018)

In the same article, Veena also "described the colors as those of the rising sun" and associated these hues with celebration and gratitude (*Statesman Journal* 1983). Taken together, the association of red with sun, celebration, and human potential combined with the movement's more liberal views on sexuality and gender roles created a dress code that viewers found inspiration-worthy in 2018 – disregarding, of course, salmonella poisoning and attempted assassinations. Further, the docuseries and subsequent interviews with those who lived at Rajneeshpuram affirmed that members did not experience the dress code as problematic or limiting. For example, Philip Toelkes (Swami Prem Niren) assured people that "their underwear did not have to be red," and that he "never found the limited palette he could wear restrictive" (Chua 2018). Unlike perceptions of the FLDS in 2008 and 2018, viewers of *Wild Wild Country* did not interpret wearing Rajneeshee red in terms of restriction, rigidity, or renunciation, which helped make their attire fashion imitation-worthy.

Further, as discussed in Section 1, the figure of the "Oriental Monk" was another reason that Rajneeshee red was acknowledged and deemed acceptable by the public in 2018, while the FLDS-prairie dress connection went incognito. Bhagwan Shree Rajneesh fulfilled Western visual expectations associated with Iwamura's concept of the "Oriental Monk" – men from the East who possessed the mystical knowledge necessary to enliven a spiritually dead West (Wuthnow 1998: 140; Iwamura 2011: 6, 20). As a guru from India adorned in beautiful robes with matching knit hats, he embodied the sartorial expectations for an enlightened spiritual guide (see Figure 27). "He certainly looked the part of the sage," according to at least one former member interviewed in the documentary. Further, his teachings affirmed this interpretation of him. Scholar Hugh Urban

Figure 27 A photograph of Bhagwan Shree Rajneesh wearing teal-colored robes with matching knit hat and a gold watch, taken in 1985. Photo courtesy of Bettmann/Getty Images.

highlights how Rajneesh's combination of Buddhism, post-Freudian psychoanalysis, and sexual liberation attracted numerous followers. In addition, the guru's sense of humor and embrace of luxury along with his critiques of religious and political institutions endeared him to many (Urban 2018). The attire worn by the Rajneesh emphasized the exotic and seemingly pure inspiration for his teachings and thus that of his followers.

Throughout, *Wild Wild Country* clearly depicts the leaders of the Rajneeshee movement, including Ma Anand Sheela, Ma Shanti B, and others – rather than the rank-and-file members – as those responsible for the group's problematic decision-making and violent actions. In contrast, ordinary Rajneeshees appear heroic and loyal. The Rajneeshees' devotion to wearing red not only showed their dedication to buying and/or dying red clothes, but it also demonstrated their willingness to endure persecution and hardship. By dressing in red, the followers of Rajneesh boldly and visibly declared their commitment, despite the disapproval and disdain of the Oregon citizens living outside Rajneeshpuram. Heightened antagonism accompanied the growth of the settlement and the Rajneeshees' involvement in local and state politics. In this atmosphere of increasing hostility, as one follower said, "you can't hide in red" (Harkavy 1984). While this statement was intended to contrast the intentional living and vibrancy of the Rajneesh community against the beige blah living of others, it also highlighted how the Rajneeshee dress code made them obvious to outsiders as hostilities and threats of violence swirled. Congressional candidate Larryann Willis called the Rajneeshees "red-clad kooks" and insisted they were not victims of bigotry and persecution, but, rather, the perpetrators of it (*The World* 1983). Another observer criticized Governor Vic Atiyeh for creating "a climate of hate," where citizens felt justified calling for the expulsion of the Rajneeshees and threatening violence. "Bumper stickers and billboards showed Rajneesh's head circled in the crosshairs of a rifle sight," and "Handbills said, 'There will be an open season on the Rajneesh, known locally as Red Vermin. These Red Rats may be a little rough to dress and if gut shot, probably not worth it'" (Smith 1990). With bumper stickers proclaiming, "Better dead than red" and people wearing "Bhagwan-buster" and "Nuke the Guru" T-shirts (see Figure 28), the Rajneeshees' commitment to wearing red displayed their dedication, loyalty, and bravery (*Statesman Journal* 1984; Chua 2018). While not blameless in the escalating rhetoric between locals and Rajneesh leadership, the Rajneeshees appear brave and idealistic, even if misguided, which also helped position Rajneeshee red as fashion worth emulating.

In addition, the docuseries aired at a time when monochromatic clothing was beginning to trend again in fashion, which fueled interest in Rajneeshee attire. *The Wall Street Journal* reported that "the fashion zeitgeist is coincidentally reflecting the cult's nearly monochromatic head-to-toe aesthetic," and cited

Figure 28 An anti-Rajneesh T-shirt that threatens to destroy Rajneeshpuram and Bhagwan Shree Rajneesh with a bomb. For more on T-shirts and religious intolerance, see Neal (2014b). Photo courtesy of Hugh B. Urban, T-shirt from the Rajneesh Artifacts and Ephemera Collection, Coll 275, University of Oregon Libraries Special Collections and University Archives.

"cult-ish" looks from different designers (Gallagher 2018). Emilia Petrarca, a senior fashion editor at *The Cut* in 2018, echoed this interpretation. She explains, "the results [Rajneeshee attire] feel oddly on-trend for 2018, which perhaps explains why the look has garnered so many responses online. Personally, I've been dressing like a Rajneeshee for years without even knowing it" (2018a). Like Gallagher, she goes on to cite recent monochromatic fashion collections. Both also highlight the resonances between cults and fashion. Gallagher highlights the language of cult ("cult of Gucci" and "cult of Balenciaga") and explains, "More than simply buying clothes, today, people are buying into a tribe." Petrarca asks, "what is fashion but a bit of a cult itself? Not only does the fashion world encourage devotion to brands, creative leaders, influencers and (divine) objects, but fashion people constantly use the term 'cult' to classify trends." Gallagher goes on to highlight people's loyalty to their cult or tribe of choice, while Petrarca concludes her piece with a more personal reflection. "I think I understand why [followers of Rajneesh wear red]. The truth is, like escaping society for the wilderness of Oregon, monochrome feels like a way to radically simplify and focus your life – an ideal look for a cult of one."

While Petrarca already sported monochromatic outfits in red hues, others were inspired to do so by the fashion trend and *Wild Wild Country*. A month after the docuseries debuted on Netflix, *The Cut* reported that "Mandy Moore hosted a Girls' Weekend Inspired by *Wild Wild Country*." On social media, Moore reposted a promotion of Petrarca's article entitled "I Want This Cult's Look" and shared her sentiments: "Same." Subsequent Instagram posts of Moore celebrating her birthday with friends show them all wearing stylish red and orange outfits with the hashtag "Yes our color palette was inspired by Rajneeshpuram." After chronicling the weekend's luxurious events, the article ends with a question: "How do we join?" (Moore 2018; Petrarca 2018b). While the media depicted Moore's Rajneeshee-clad girls' weekend as idyllic, the Rajneesh-inspired Halloween costumes donned by Kate Hudson and her friends garnered a different reaction. Hudson posted a picture of her and the group in Rajneeshee red along with a quote from Rajneesh, "Don't be worried about the future. Live this moment so totally that the next moment comes out of it golden" (Hudson 2018). While many liked Hudson's post, a vocal subset criticized it for not acknowledging the wrongdoings committed by the community and its leaders. Still others condemned it for "making light" of the group's tumultuous history in Oregon. As one poster commented, "this group committed bioterrorism against my home state. This was really, in poor taste. Cults aren't cool, Kate" (Baila 2018; Hudson 2018; Yam 2018). It is important to remember that those inspired by Rajneeshee red and monochromatic dressing, as with the prairie dress wearers of 2018 – whether celebrities or not – did so without the risks, perceptions, and stereotypes that Rajneeshees and FLDS women faced. Nor did they experience the same type of "moral demand," individually or collectively, by doing so (Goffman 1959: 13). Wearing one's faith comes with a host of expectations and norms that do not apply when people, such as Moore, Petrarca, and Hudson, don Rajneeshee red or wear monochromatic outfits. Putting on a red dress for a weekend or slipping into a Rajneesh-inspired costume may draw temporary admiration or criticism, but the next day you wear different outfits, and the media moves on.

This case study highlights a few important facets of the cult–fashion relationship; namely, the notable impact of social media and streaming on fashion and our view of NRMs. Unlike the prairie dress, the public's fascination with the docuseries and Rajneeshee red (rather than with specific designers like Hay) drove interest in monochromatic trends. It seems likely that without the docuseries, fashion critics would have noted that monochromatic dress was trending and little else. However, with the rise of streaming, social media, and podcasts in the twenty-first century, the public has more influence than ever on fashion trends and cycles. As scholars have long argued, fashion is not simply a trickle-down enterprise (Entwistle 2000: 223). At the same time, these platforms, whether Instagram or Netflix, a true crime podcast or YouTube video, function as some of the strongest purveyors of stereotypical cult content. Historically, cult-inspired programming in fictional and informational television has been immensely popular (Neal 2011), so its continued popularity on social media and through new streaming services and genres such as the docuseries should come as no surprise. Further, the fascination with Rajneeshee red illustrates that some cults are deemed more fashionable than others based on a formula that factors in superficial perceptions of a given movement's theology and history, assessments of the authenticity of its leaders and followers, conceptualizations of religious exoticism and purity, and the immediate context surrounding its oppositional dress. To put this another way, is the group interpreted as liberal or conservative? Is it alien yet cool? Unfamiliar but aligned with popular tastes? Lastly, despite the popularity of the monochromatic dress of the Rajneeshees, this did little to disrupt or challenge the hegemonic cult stereotype. As the Instagram poster reminded actress Kate Hudson, "cults aren't cool" (Sidley 2018).

Conclusion

Examining the popularity of prairie dresses and Rajneeshee red in 2018 demonstrates that there is no simple linear cause and effect relationship between cults and fashion. Rarely is there a direct connection where a fashion designer identifies a specific cult as their inspiration; rather, these ideas and influences – news coverage, social media, the internet, popular TV, film, and docuseries, and subcultures – flow through different nodes and branches. As forms of communication continue to proliferate, it will be important to consider how they are used to uphold and/or challenge ideas about NRMs.

It may be helpful, then, to revisit, and perhaps revise, sociologist Anson Shupe's five stages of perception and labeling in relation to religious groups deemed evil or cults. During the "latent, presconstruction" phase, the NRM is perceived by the public as one of many such groups, but largely ignored. The "benign construction" stage features media coverage characterized as "positive, if slightly eccentric," which is followed by "skeptical construction," which usually occurs after some catalyzing event that prompts more scrutiny and negative views of these groups fueled by concerned relatives and former members. In the fourth and most common phase, "accepted malicious construction," the coverage is "overwhelmingly negative and cynical" as it assumes and fuels the cult stereotype and is accepted by most as fact. The last stage, "postmalicious construction," which occurs after NRMs are not deemed to be a threat and NRM-related controversies have faded, features laughter, jokes, and parodies (Shupe 1987). Shupe's stages capture the general arc of media coverage; however, with the proliferation of communication and social media technologies, how might we re-envision and complicate Shupe's analysis to better capture our current mediated landscape? Is fashion's embrace of the prairie dress and Rajneeshee red part of the postmalicious construction phase that assures consumer-citizens that ultimately these groups are harmless, or should we add another phase to Shupe's schema?

These case studies also highlight the complex ways that cults and fashion, as well as the broader discourse of religion, intersect. The fashion industry, as we have seen, often incorporates the oppositional fashion of marginalized groups and subcultures, religious and otherwise. The faithful devotion and dress work of the FLDS and the Rajneeshees becomes the fashionable attire of 2018. Sometimes designers explicitly acknowledge their inspirations and other times they do not. However, even as cult styles become incorporated into mainstream fashion, the stereotype persists and differentiates these groups from religions accepted as normative. As a result, we need to examine and analyze how fashion, along with other industries and media forms, contributes to building and maintaining the boundaries that protect the discourse of religion.

Lastly, these case studies point to the need for more research. We should investigate other moments and events in the cult–fashion relationship that will enrich our understanding. For example, scholar Kayla Renée Wheeler argues that we need to consider how women of the NOI have been "erased from Muslim fashion narratives." She explains, "by emphasizing the relatively new embrace of modest fashion by the mainstream fashion industry, we run the risk of ignoring the Black Muslim trailblazers who helped make the rise of such fashion possible" (Wheeler 2021, 2023). We also should consider how some NRMs provided women and men with the space to experiment with and create their own clothing and fashions. For example, Sister Ethel Sharrieff designed beautiful modest gowns that were photographed for *Muhammad Speaks* in 1962, and founded the clothing factory and store in Chicago (Clothing Factory; Wheeler 2023), FLDS women created FLDSDress.com, the Rajneeshees bought and sold red-hued clothes, and Mormon fashion influencers have gained tremendous popularity in recent years. These and other case studies call for further research and examination into how people fashion and wear their faith.

4 Concluding Thoughts

Many people across religious traditions wear their faith, whether clothing or jewelry or both. From habits to hijab, Christian cross jewelry to Star of David pendants, religion and clothing are intertwined, rather than separate, realms. These forms of attire and adornment constitute a vital way people create, live, and foster their religious identities. "Belief," argues scholar David Morgan, "happens in and through things and what people do with them" (2005: 8). People literally and figuratively wear their faith and in doing so enliven their traditions. This applies to most religions, as well as groups labeled cults. When studying NRMs and religion more broadly, we need to attend to the materiality of their practices. As scholar Meredith McGuire argues, "Our discipline has been impoverished by the fact that it has been so heavily influenced by an epistemological tradition, itself a cultural and historical construction, in which things of the spirit have been radically split from material things, and in which the mind is considered separate from body" (1990: 284). Our knowledge of NRMs will be enriched by researching and learning about their clothes and other forms of material culture.

Further, and apparent throughout this Element, we must continue to question and critique the hegemonic cult stereotype as it hinders us from identifying commonalities across faith traditions and prevents us from gaining in-depth knowledge about them. Gaining knowledge about these groups is more important now than ever given the proliferation of social media, podcasts, and streaming, technologies that thrive on stereotypes and soundbites. We need to be active interpreters, analysts, and critics of our media and our media consumption.

In *Wearing Their Faith*, we have seen the centrality of wearing distinct forms of dress in a variety of NRMs. Complex dress work helps create charismatic leaders and form faithful followers. For leaders, dress work helps establish authority and legitimacy, while it fosters identity and belonging in followers. This sense of belonging may look stifling to some, but abiding by a dress code or other forms of wearing one's faith are not zero-sum games of oppression or liberation. Rather, people often find dress work to be a vital source of meaning and empowerment even as they navigate the structural constraints and obstacles that shape their lives. We have only touched on a few case studies in this Element and more research needs to be done so that we can better understand the dress work of NRMs and other religions.

We must also continue to research and analyze the fashion industry, especially as it pertains to religious traditions, histories, and symbols, including those of NRMs. Was the cult fashion moment of 2018 with the popularity of prairie dresses and Rajneeshee red an isolated instance or will we see more intersections between NRMs, dress, and fashion in the future? As fashion designers continually seek inspiration and attention, will groups labeled cults become a more frequently used repository of symbols and styles? Will, as we saw in Section 3, a hierarchy of seemingly more-acceptable NRMs emerge that are seen as fashion inspiration-worthy, while others continue to be derided? How might these continued NRM–fashion interactions uphold or challenge the cult stereotype? Further, if we see an increase in interactions and intersections of NRMs, religion, and fashion, what are the implications as we think about the ethics of religious and cultural appropriation? What does it mean to wear someone else's faith?

References

ABC News. (2015). New Wave of Mormon Missionaries Is Young, Energetic and Female. *ABCNews.go.com*, January 27. abcnews.go.com/US/wave-mormon-missionaries-young-energetic-female/story?id=27924269 (accessed May 22, 2024).

ACLU. (2008). Texas Supreme Court Calls Removal of Children from Yearning for Zion Ranch "Unwarranted." *ACLU.org*, May 29. www.aclu.org/press-releases/texas-supreme-court-calls-removal-children-yearning-zion-ranch-unwarranted (accessed March 25, 2024).

Alvi, S. S., Hoodfar, H. & McDonough, S., eds. (2003). *The Muslim Veil in North America: Issues and Debates*. Toronto: Women's Press.

Ames Daily Tribune (Ames, Iowa). (1975). Maharishi: Iowa Could Become the "First Ideal State in the World," March 27, p. 18.

Arthur, L. B. (1999). Introduction. In L. B. Berg, ed., *Religion, Dress and the Body*. Oxford: Berg, pp. 1–8.

Baila, M. (2018). Yes, Your *Wild Wild Country* Costume Is Offensive – Here's Why. *Refinery29.com*, October 31. www.refinery29.com/en-us/2018/10/209209/wild-wild-country-cult-costumes (accessed March 12, 2024).

Baker, K. J. (n.d.) Fashionable Intolerance, *Sacred Matters Magazine*. sacredmattersmagazine.com/fashionable-intolerance/ (accessed March 18, 2024).

Baker, K. J. (2008). Religious Dress. In H. Sheumaker & S. T. Wajda, eds., *Material Culture in America: Understanding Everyday Life*. Santa Barbara, CA: ABC-CLIO, pp. 388–90. *Gale eBooks* (accessed September 26, 2022).

Barnard, M. (1996). *Fashion as Communication*. London: Routledge.

Beckford, R. (2009). Black Suit Matters: Faith, Politics, and Religious Representation in the Religious Documentary. In A. Pinn, ed., *Black Religion and Aesthetics: Religious Thought and Life in Africa and the African Diaspora*. New York: Palgrave Macmillan, pp. 135–51.

Berman, J. (2008). Get Ready for Prairie Chic! *Salon.com*, July 1. www.salon.com/2008/07/01/prairie_chic/ (accessed March 14, 2024).

Blythe, C. J. (2014). The Coronation of James J. Strang and the Making of Beaver Island Mormonism. *Communal Societies* 34(1). https://link.gale.com/apps/doc/A474768199/AONE?u=nclivewfuy&sid=bookmark-AONE&xid=b9b5717d.

Borowik, C. (2023). *From Radical Jesus People to Virtual Religion: The Family International*. New York: Cambridge University Press.

References

Breward, C. (2016). *The Suit: Form, Function & Style*. London: Reaktion Books.

Bromley, D. (2014). Charisma and Leadership: Charisma and Charismatic Authority in New Religious Movements. In G. D. Chryssides & B. E. Zeller, eds., *The Bloomsbury Companion to New Religious Movements*. London: Bloomsbury, pp. 103–17.

Brownie, B. (2019). *Spacewear: Weightlessness and the Final Frontier of Fashion*. London: Bloomsbury Visual Arts. http://dx.doi.org/10.5040/9781350000353.ch-001.

Bucar, E. (2017). *Pious Fashion: How Muslim Women Dress*. Cambridge, MA: Harvard University Press.

Buck, J. (1968). Indian "Guru" Urges "Inner Peace" to End Fighting. *The Idaho Statesman*. Boise, Idaho, January 21, 8A.

Calvert, L. 2024. Personal Communication, Zoom Interview, 23 April.

CBS News. (2008). Why Do They Dress That Way? *CBSNews.com*, April 18. www.cbsnews.com/news/why-do-they-dress-that-way/ (accessed March 18, 2024).

The Central New Jersey Home News. (1942). The Problem is Serious, August 23, p. 4.

Chancellor, J. D. (2000). *Life in the Family: An Oral History of the Children of God*. Syracuse, NY: Syracuse University Press.

Chidester, D. (1988). *Salvation and Suicide: Jim Jones, the Peoples Temple, and Jonestown*. Bloomington: Indiana University Press.

Chowdury, N. (2018). Dressing Like You're in a Cult is Next Season's Most Covetable Fashion Trend. *Elle (Australia)*, November 5. www.elle.com.au/fashion/fashion-news/cult-fashion-18795/ (accessed August 18, 2022).

Christensen, D. R. (2005). Inventing L. Ron Hubbard: On the Construction and Maintenance of the Hagiographic Mythology of Scientology's Founder. In J. R. Lewis & J. A. Petersen, eds., *Controversial New Religions*. Oxford: Oxford University Press, 2005, pp. 227–58.

Chua, J. M. (2018). The Story behind *Wild Wild Country*'s Red Rajneeshee Outfits. *Racked.com*, April 16. www.racked.com/2018/4/16/17235638/wild-wild-country-rajneeshee-red-rajneespuram-maroon-burgundy-orange (accessed March 12, 2024).

The Church of Jesus Christ of Latter-Day Saints. (n.d.). Chastity. *ChurchofJesusChrist.org*, www.churchofjesuschrist.org/study/manual/true-to-the-faith/chastity?lang=eng#title1 (accessed February 5, 2024).

References

The Church of Jesus Christ of Latter-Day Saints. (n.d.). Dress and Appearance. *ChurchofJesusChrist.org*, www.churchofjesuschrist.org/callings/missionary/dress-and-appearance?lang=eng (accessed January 25, 2024).

The Church of Jesus Christ of Latter-Day Saints. (n.d.). Guidelines for Elders. *ChurchofJesusChrist.org*, www.churchofjesuschrist.org/callings/missionary/guidelines-for-elders?lang=eng (accessed January 25, 2024).

The Church of Jesus Christ of Latter-Day Saints. (n.d.). Missionary Standards for Disciples of Jesus Christ. *ChurchofJesusChrist.org*, www.churchofjesuschrist.org/study/manual/missionary-standards-for-disciples-of-jesus-christ?lang=eng (accessed January 22, 2024).

Cooke, P. (n.d.). Children of God Memoir. *Making Sense of Cults*, makingsenseofcults.com/children-of-god/ (accessed January 23, 2024).

Corrigan, J. & Neal, L. S. (2020). *Religious Intolerance in America: A Documentary History*, 2nd ed. Chapel Hill: University of North Carolina Press.

Cowan, D. E. and Bromley, D. G. (2015). *Cults and New Religions: A Brief History*, 2nd ed. Malden, MA: Wiley Blackwell.

Curtis IV, E. E. (2002). Islamizing the Black Body: Ritual and Power in Elijah Muhammad's Nation of Islam. *Religion and American Culture* 12(2), pp. 167–96.

Cusack, A. (2004). Sun Myung Moon Crowned Messiah in Washington, DC. *AndrewCusack.com,* June 14. www.andrewcusack.com/2004/sun-myung-moon-crowned-messiah-in-washington-dc/ (accessed May 22, 2024).

Dart, J. (1970). "Children of God" Sect Resurrects Doom Prophecy. *The Los Angeles Times*, August 2, pp. 9B, 8C.

Dasi, S. D. (2020). The Divine Love Trip, Part 84, *HareKrsna.com*, www.harekrsna.com/sun/editorials/02-21/editorials18607.htm (accessed April 1, 2024).

The David Letterman Show. (1982–1991). Eccentric Civilian Guests Collection on Letterman, 1982–1991. *YouTube.com*, youtu.be/FN-oMk4dzBQ (accessed March 28, 2024).

Davis, D. with Davis, B. (1984). *The Children of God: The Inside Story by the Daughter of the Founder, Moses David*, www.exfamily.org/art/exmem/debdavis/debdavis06.shtml (accessed January 23, 2024).

Detroit Free Press. (1934). U.S. May Fight Voodoo in City, April 18, p. 23.

Dillon, J. & Richardson, J. (1994). The "Cult" Concept: A Politics of Representation Analysis. *Syzygy: Journal of Alternative Religion and Culture* 3, pp. 185–97.

Divine, M. (1950). Life with Father, *Ebony*, December, pp. 52–60.

Dorman, J. H. (1988). Shaping the Popular Image of Post-Reconstruction American Blacks: The "Coon Song" Phenomenon of the Gilded Age. *American Quarterly* 40(4), pp. 450–71.

Durham, M. G. (2001). Displaced Persons: Symbols of South Asian Femininity and the Returned Gaze in U.S. Media Culture. *Communication Theory* 11(2), pp. 201–17.

Dwyer-McNulty, S. (2014). *Common Threads: A Cultural History of Clothing in American Catholicism*. Chapel Hill: University of North Carolina Press.

Edwards, L. (2009). Beaver Island's Mormon King, James Strang. *MyNorth.com*, March 20. mynorth.com/2009/03/beaver-islands-king/ (accessed October 31, 2022).

Emberley, J. (2010). Fur. In V. Steele, ed., *The Berg Companion to Fashion*. Oxford: Bloomsbury Academic, pp. 353–55. http://dx.doi.org/10.5040/9781474264716.0007724 (accessed October 31, 2022).

Entwistle, J. (2000). *The Fashioned Body: Fashion, Dress and Modern Social Theory*. Cambridge: Polity Press.

Farrell, A. (2019). Sect and the City: The Peculiar Allure of the Prairie Dress. *FT.com*, July 26. wake.idm.oclc.org/login?url=https://www.proquest.com/trade-journals/sect-city-peculiar-allure-prairie-dress/docview/2264509498/se-2 (accessed March 18, 2024).

Finley, S. C. (2022). *In & Out of This World: Material and Extraterrestrial Bodies in the Nation of Islam*. Durham: Duke University Press.

Fischer, F. (1971). Dedication with a Beat. *The Shreveport Journal*, September 9, pp. 1B, 2B.

Friedman, V. (2017). Women, Fashion Has You Covered. *NYTimes.com*, April 6. www.nytimes.com/2017/04/06/fashion/covered-up-fashion-style-of-the-decade.html (accessed March 18, 2024).

Gallagher, J. (2018). The Latest Fashion Trend? Dressing Like You're in a Cult. *The Wall Street Journal*, April 2. www.wsj.com/articles/the-latest-fashion-trend-dressing-like-youre-in-a-cult-1522688672 (accessed March 25, 2024).

Gibson, D. M. & Karim, J. (2014). *Women of the Nation: Between Black Protest and Sunni Islam*. New York: New York University Press.

Givhan, R. (2008). The Flamboyance of Simplicity. *WashingtonPost.com*, April 25, www.washingtonpost.com/wp-dyn/content/article/2008/04/25/AR2008042500927.html (accessed March 18, 2024).

Givhan, R. (2018a). Fanny Packs. Prairie Dresses. Luxury Shower Shoes: Is Fashion Trolling Us or What? *Washingtonpost.com*, July 19. www.washingtonpost.com/lifestyle/style/fanny-packs-prairie-dresses-luxury-shower-shoes-is-fashion-trolling-us-or-what/2018/07/19/acdc46a6-7edf-11e8-bb6b-c1cb691f1402_story.html (accessed March 19, 2024).

Givhan, R. (2018b). Prairie Dresses – Yes, Prairie Dresses – Are the Most Provocative Thing in Fashion Right Now. *WashingtonPost.com*, September 13. www.washingtonpost.com/news/arts-and-entertainment/wp/2018/09/13/prairie-dresses-yes-prairie-dresses-are-the-most-provocative-thing-in-fashion-right-now/ (accessed March 14, 2024).

Goffman, E. (1959). *The Presentation of Self in Everyday Life*. New York: Anchor Books.

Goldman, M. S. (2005). Rajneesh. In L. Jones, ed., *Encyclopedia of Religion*, 2nd ed., vol. 11. Detroit, MI: Macmillan Reference USA, pp. 7608–7609.

Gordon, S. B. & Shipps, J. (2011). A New Mormon Moment. *The New York Times*, July 4, www.nytimes.com/roomfordebate/2011/07/04/are-republicans-ready-now-for-a-mormon-president/a-new-mormon-moment (accessed January 25, 2024).

Gorenfeld, J. (2004). Hail to the Moon King. *Salon.com*, June 21. www.salon.com/2004/06/21/moon_7/ (accessed April 1, 2024).

Goswami, T. K. & Gupta, R. M. (2005). Krishna and Culture: What Happens When the Lord of Vrindavana Moves to New York City. In T. A. Forsthoefel and C. A. Humes, eds., *Gurus in America*. Ithaca: Ithaca State University of New York Press, pp. 81–95.

Grace, J. H. (1985). *Sex and Marriage in the Unification Movement*. New York: Edwin Mellen Press.

Graybill, B. & Arthur, L. B. (1999). The Social Control of Women's Bodies in Two Mennonite Communities. In L. B. Arthur, ed., *Religion, Dress and the Body*, Oxford: Berg, pp. 9–30.

Grazian, D. (2010). Demystifying Authenticity in the Sociology of Culture. In L. Grindstaff, M. M. Lo, & J. R. Hall, eds. *Handbook of Cultural Sociology*. London: Routledge, pp. 191–200.

Hall, S. (1997). *Representation: Cultural Representations and Signifying Practices*. London: SAGE.

Harkavy, W. (1984). Guru, Guns and Money. *Arizona Republic*, September 23, pp. A1, A14.

Harris, S. with Crittenden, H. (1953). *Father Divine: Holy Husband*. New York: Doubleday.

Harvard University. (n.d.). The Rush of Gurus. *The Pluralism Project*. pluralism.org/the-rush-of-gurus (accessed April 1, 2024).

Herman, A. (2018). "Wild Wild Country" Is Not Your Average Cult Exposé. *The Ringer*, March 27. www.theringer.com/tv/2018/3/27/17166926/wild-wild-country-netflix (accessed March 13, 2024).

Hill Collins, P. (1990). *Black Feminist Thought*. New York: Routledge.

Hollander, A. (1978). *Seeing Through Clothes*. New York: The Viking Press.

Hume, L. (2013). *Religious Life of Dress: Global Fashion and Faith*. London: Bloomsbury Academic.

Humes, C. A. (2005). Maharishi Mahesh Yogi: Beyond the TM Technique. In T. A. Forsthoefel and C. A. Humes, eds., *Gurus in America*. Ithaca: State University of New York Press, pp. 55–79.

Hudson, K. (2018). Photo of Rajneeshee-Inspired Halloween Costumes. *Instagram*, October 28, 2018. www.instagram.com/p/BpfcliRgcPo/ (accessed April 9, 2024).

Hyland, V. (2015). Introducing Cultcore: A Caftan for Every Day of the Week. *The Cut*, September 21. www.thecut.com/2015/09/cultcore.html (accessed February 6, 2024).

Ingram, A. (2020). Church Announces New Dress Standards for Elder Missionaries. *LDS Daily,* June 12. www.ldsdaily.com/church-lds/church-announces-new-dress-standards-for-elder-missionaries/ (accessed January 25, 2024).

Iwamura, J. N. (2011). *Virtual Orientalism: Asian Religions and American Popular Culture*. New York: Oxford University Press.

Joseph, N. (1986). *Uniforms and Nonuniforms: Communication through Clothing*. New York: Greenwood Press.

Kaiser, S. B. & Looysen, R. (2010). Antifashion. In P. G. Tortora, ed., *Berg Encyclopedia of World Dress and Fashion: The United States and Canada*. Oxford: Bloomsbury Academic, pp. 160–70. http://dx.doi.org/10.2752/BEWDF/EDch3023.

Kamboj, P. (2018). "Vaishnava Dress" Really Exists and ISKCON Devotees Must Wear It. *Akincana Goca*, August 22. akincana.net/2018/08/22/vaishnava-dress-really-exists-and-iskcon-devotees-must-wear-it/ (accessed April 1, 2024).

Karapanagiotis, N. (2021). *Branding Bhakti: Krishna Consciousness and the Makeover of a Movement*. Bloomington: Indiana University Press.

Karefa-Johnson, G. (2018). An Entire Wardrobe Inspired by the Rajneeshee Movement of 'Wild Wild Country.' *Garage.vice.com*, April 5. Accessed August 18, 2022. Article now offline.

Keenan, W. (1999). From Friars to Fornicators: The Eroticization of Sacred Dress. *Fashion Theory* 3(4), pp. 389–410.

Ketola, K. (2008). *The Founder of the Hare Krishnas as Seen by Devotees: A Cognitive Study of Religious Charisma*. Leiden, Boston: Brill.

King, J. (2017). Clearing the Planet: Dianetics Auditing and the Eschatology of the Nation of Islam. In D. M. Gibson & H. Berg, eds., *New Perspectives on the Nation of Islam*. London: Taylor & Francis Group, pp. 218–35.

Kyvig, D. E. (2002). Everett Dirksen's Constitutional Crusades. *Journal of the Illinois State Historical Society* 95(1), pp. 68–85.

LA Times. (1985). Followers Allowed to Stop Wearing Red: Guru Renounces Book of Rajneeshism. *LATimes Archives*, September 27. www.latimes.com/archives/la-xpm-1985-09-27-mn-18112-story.html (accessed August 18, 2022).

Lindsey, R. M. (2014). "Seen and Read of Men": Biblical Text and the Living Epistles of Father Divine's Peace Mission Movement. *Journal of Africana Religions* 2(3), pp. 347–78.

Lo, D. (2008). Latter-Day Restraints. *NYPost.com*, April 22. nypost.com/2008/04/22/latter-day-restraints/ (accessed March 18, 2024).

Lodi, M. (2016). Uriel, the Universe's Best Dressed Spiritual Leader. *Racked*, January 29. www.racked.com/2016/1/29/10850646/unarius-ufo-reincarnation-cosmic-uriel (accessed March 28, 2024).

Maira, M. (2002). Temporary Tattoos: Indo-Chic Fantasies and Late Capitalist Orientalism. *Meridians* 3(1), pp. 134–60.

McCormick, P. (2008). Healing Colonial Trauma: Marcus Garvey, Cargo Movements, and Symbolic Empowerment. *Journal of Black Studies* 39(2), pp. 252–65.

McDannell, C. (1995). *Material Christianity: Religion and Popular Culture in America*. New Haven, CT: Yale University Press.

McGeown, J. (2019). Elizabethan Sumptuary Laws: Fashion Policing in Shakespeare's England. www.shakespearesglobe.com/discover/blogs-and-features/2019/04/16/elizabethan-sumptuary-laws-fashion-policing-in-shakespeares-england/ (accessed October 31, 2022).

McGuire, M. B. (1990). Religion and the Body: Rematerializing the Human Body in the Social Sciences of Religion. *Journal for the Scientific Study of Religion* 29(3), pp. 283–96.

The Miami Herald. (1982). Moon Marries 5,387 Couples – All at Once, October 15, p. 22A.

Michel, L. (2018). The *Wild Wild Country* Directors Explain How They Made Their Shocking Cult Documentary. *GQ.com*, March 29. www.gq.com/story/wild-wild-country-directors-interview (accessed March 26, 2024).

Mickler, M. L. (2022). *The Unification Church Movement*. New York: Cambridge University Press.

"Minimal Loss" (2005). *Criminal Minds* Season 4, Episode 3. Directed and written by Danny Cannon. CBS, October 13.

The Montreal Gazette. (1972). Maharishi Tells Queen's Students to Continue Short-Hair Culture, August 2, p. 17.

Moore, M. (2018). Photo of Girls' Weekend at Alila Ventana Big Sur. *Instagram*, April 15. www.instagram.com/p/Bhm-dM5H-EP/?img_index=1 (accessed March 25, 2024).

Morgan, D. (2005). *The Sacred Gaze: Religious Visual Culture in Theory and Practice*. Berkeley: University of California Press.

Morgan, D. (2010). Introduction. In D. Morgan, ed., *Religion and Material Culture: The Matter of Belief*. London: Routledge, pp. 1–17.

Moton, S. (1966). What the Teachings of the Messenger Mean to Women. *Muhammad Speaks* June 3, p. 25.

Muhammad, E. (1968). Warning to M.G.T. and G.C. Class. *Muhammad Speaks*, June 28, p. 4.

Muhammad, E. (1970). To the Black Woman in America. *Muhammad Speaks*, September 4, pp. 16–17.

Muhammad Speaks. (1962). Clothing Factory Big Step Forward, February, pp. 16–17.

Muhammad Speaks. (1967). Indecency in Female Dress Still Not Tolerated in Islam, March 3, p. 19.

Muhammad Speaks. (1968). The Filth of the Filth, June 28, p. 3.

NBC News. (2008). Polygamists Make Their Own Fashion Statement. *NBCNews.com*, April 21. www.nbcnews.com/id/wbna24245576 (accessed March 18, 2024).

Neal, L. S. (2011). "They're Freaks!": The Cult Stereotype in Fictional Television Shows, 1958–2008. *Nova Religio* 14(3), 81–107.

Neal, L. S. (2014a). Rescripting the Past: Suicide Cults on Television. In J. R. Lewis & C. M. Cusack, eds., *Sacred Suicide*. Burlington, VT: Ashgate, pp. 253–69.

Neal, L. S. (2014b). The Ideal Democratic Apparel: T-shirts, Religious Intolerance, and the Clothing of Democracy. *Material Religion* 10(2), pp. 182–207.

Neal, L. S. (2019). *Religion in Vogue: Christianity and Fashion in America*. New York: New York University Press.

Norcross, H. (2019). BYU Women Face Social Pressure to Serve Full-Time Missions, *The Daily Universe*, April 30. universe.byu.edu/2019/04/30/final-project/ (accessed April 1, 2024).

Oakland Tribune. (1937). Father Divine Out on Bail; "Peace" Returns to Harlem, April 23, p. D3.

Olivelle, P. (2005). The Renouncer Tradition. In G. Flood, ed., *The Blackwell Companion to Hinduism*. Oxford: Blackwell, pp. 271–87.

O'Neal, G. (1999). The African American Church, its Sacred Cosmos, and Dress. In L. B. Arthur, ed., *Religion, Dress and the Body*, Oxford: Berg, pp. 117–34.

Palmer, S. J. and Gareau, P. (2017). Belief. In A. Palmer, ed., *A Cultural History of Dress and Fashion in the Modern Age*. London: Bloomsbury Academic, pp. 85–106. http://dx.doi.org/10.5040/9781474206402.ch-004.

Payne, L. (2015). "Pants Don't Make Preachers": Fashion and Gender Construction in Late-Nineteenth and Early-Twentieth Century American Revivalism. *Fashion Theory* 19(1), pp. 83–113.

Petrarca, E. (2018a). I Want This Cult's Look. *The Cut*, March 28. www.thecut.com/2018/03/wild-wild-country-rajneesh-clothes-monochrome.html (accessed March 14, 2024).

Petrarca, E. (2018b). Mandy Moore Hosted a Girls' Weekend Inspired by *Wild Wild Country*. *The Cut*, April 16. www.thecut.com/2018/04/mandy-moore-wild-wild-country-rajnjeeshpuram-monochrome.html (March 12, 2024).

Piela, A. (2021). *Wearing the Niqab: Muslim Women in the UK and US*. London: Bloomsbury Academic.

Pinn, A. (2009). Introduction: The Black Labyrinth, Aesthetics, and Black Religion. In A. Pinn, ed., *Black Religion and Aesthetics: Religious Thought and Life in Africa and the African Diaspora*. New York: Palgrave Macmillan, pp. 1–15.

The Post Standard (Syracuse, NY) (1970). 790 Couples Join in Mass Wedding, October 22, p. 4.

Pountain, D. & Robbins, D. (2000). *Cool Rules: Anatomy of an Attitude*. London: Reaktion Books.

Primiano, L. N. (2017). International Peace Mission Movement and Father Divine. In *The Encyclopedia of Greater Philadelphia*. philadelphiaencyclopedia.org/essays/international-peace-mission-movement-and-father-divine/ (accessed April 10, 2024).

Raes, B. (2018). Shopping with a Client Inspired by the Documentary *Wild Wild Country. BridgetteRaes.com*, October 8. www.bridgetteraes.com/2018/10/08/shopping-with-a-client-inspired-by-the-documentary-wild-wild-country/ (accessed March 18, 2024).

Ramachandran, T. (2022). Personal Interview.

Real People. (n.d.). Spaceship Ruthie | Real People | George Schlatter. *YouTube.com*, youtu.be/Ub1Z-U0d9D0 (accessed March 28, 2024).

Reed, M. C. (2016). Nation of Islam. In E. J. Blum, ed., *America in the World, 1776 to the Present: A Supplement to the Dictionary of American History* (Vol. 2). Farmington Hills, MI: Charles Scribner's Sons, pp. 716–18.

Russell, A. (2018). Batsheva Hay Rethinks the Traditions of Feminine Dress. *Newyorker.com*, September 10. www.newyorker.com/magazine/2018/09/10/batsheva-hay-rethinks-the-traditions-of-feminine-dress (accessed March 18, 2024).

Said, E. W. (1980). *Orientalism*. London: Routledge & Kegan Paul.

Sandberg, B. (2018). "Wild Wild Country" Filmmakers Reveal the One Person Who Refused to Be Interviewed. *TheHollywoodReporter.com*, June 1. www.hollywoodreporter.com/news/general-news/wild-wild-country-who-refused-be-interviewed-documentary-1114873/ (accessed March 25, 2024).

Sawyer, D. & Humes, C. (2023). *The Transcendental Meditation Movement*. New York: Cambridge University Press.

Sharrieff, B. (1968). Life in Sudan: Respect for Our Black Women. *Muhammad Speaks* June 28, p. 26.

Schmidt, L. E. (1989). A Church-Going People Are A Dress-Loving People: Clothes, Communication, and Religious Culture in Early America. *Church History* 58(1), 36–51.

Scott, E. (2016). A Perfectly Erik Lengthy Swan Song. *Elder Erik Scott Missionary Blog*, November 7. scottboys.wordpress.com/ (accessed February 5, 2024).

Shipps, J. (2000). *Sojourner in the Promised Land: Forty Years among the Mormons*. Urbana: University of Illinois Press.

Shupe, A. (1987). Constructing Evil as a Social Process: The Unification Church and the Media. In R. N. Bellah & F. E. Greenspahn, eds., *Uncivil Religion: Interreligious Hostility in America*. New York: Crossroad, pp. 205–17.

Sidley, S. B. (2018). Comment on Kate Hudson's Rajneeshee-Inspired Halloween Costumes Photo. *Instagram*, October 28. www.instagram.com/p/BpfcliRgcPo/ (accessed April 9, 2024).

Sims, S. (2010). Work and the Wardrobe: Men. In P. G. Tortora, ed., *Berg Encyclopedia of World Dress and Fashion: The United States and Canada*. Oxford: Bloomsbury Academic. http://dx.doi.org/10.5040/9781847888525.EDch031911.

Sims, A. (2018). We're So Into the *Wild Wild Country* Color Scheme and We're Not Sorry. *Architecturaldigest.com*, April 26. www.architecturaldigest.com/story/were-so-into-the-wild-wild-country-color-scheme-and-were-not-sorry (accessed March 14, 2024).

Slone, I. (2018). Why are People so Obsessed with this 1980s Cult's Style? *Fashionmagazine.com*, April 2. fashionmagazine.com/style/rajneeshee-style-wild-wild-country/ (accessed August 18, 2022).

Smith, D. (2022). Tanning & Meditating on Deer Skin. *Vital Veda*, October 4. vitalveda.com.au/learn/tanning-and-meditating-on-deer-skin/ (accessed April 10, 2024).

Smith, K. (1990). Oregon Bigots. *The Burlington (Vt.) Free Press* February 20, p. 9A.

SMU Jones Film. (1973). The Children of God Hold a Vigil to Warn People of a Disaster in the Next 40 Days. *YouTube.com*. youtu.be/tFtu5rt6WS0?si=c5Lo8eT9DOuIJBdb (accessed April 3, 2024).

Stark, R. (1987). How New Religions Succeed: A Theoretical Model. In D. G. Bromley & P. E. Hammond, eds., *The Future of New Religious Movements*. Macon, GA: Mercer University Press, pp. 11–29.

Statesman Journal (Salem Oregon). (1983). Rajneesh Color Represents "Flaming" Human Potential, July 3, p. 56

Statesman Journal (Salem Oregon). (1984). Rajneeshees, Foes Targets of Calls, Flood of Hate Mail, November 4, p. 11D.

Stolberg, S. G. (2004). A Crowning at the Capital Creates a Stir. *The New York Times*, June 24. www.nytimes.com/2004/06/24/us/a-crowning-at-the-capital-creates-a-stir.html (accessed April 1, 2024).

Sturken, M. (1997). *Tangled Memories: The Vietnam War, the AIDS Epidemic, and the Politics of Remembering*. Berkeley: University of California Press.

Sunhak Institute of History. (1962). Father and Mother Bless the 72-Couple Blessing Group on June 4. history.familyfed.org/photo/72-couple-blessing-group-1962 (accessed April 2, 2024).

Sunhak Institute of History. (1969). European Blessing of Eight Couples, Essen, Germany on March 28. history.familyfed.org/photo/european-blessing-8-couples (accessed April 2, 2024).

Synnott, A. (1987). Shame and Glory: A Sociology of Hair. *The British Journal of Sociology* 38(3), pp. 381–413.

Taylor, U. Y. (2017). *The Promise of Patriarchy: Women and the Nation of Islam*. Chapel Hill: The University of North Carolina Press.

Tribe, S. (2023). The Tiaras of the Popes: Pope Pius XI. *Liturgical Arts Journal* April 21. www.liturgicalartsjournal.com/2023/04/the-tiaras-of-popes-pope-pius-xi.html (accessed April 3, 2024).

Tumminia, D. G. (2005). *When Prophecy Never Fails: Myth and Reality in a Flying-Saucer Group*. Oxford: Oxford University Press.

Unarius Academy of Science. (n.d.). Creativity for AVAM. *YouTube.com*, youtu.be/FL65rpg_TJ0 (accessed March 28, 2024).

Unarius Academy of Science. (2020). Interplanetary Confederation Day 2020 Pt. 3. *YouTube.com*, youtu.be/WL1GsGgjvEQ (accessed March 28, 2024).

Urban, H. B. (2015). *Zorba the Buddha: Sex, Spirituality, and Capitalism in the Global Osho Movement*. Berkeley: University of California Press.

Urban, H. B. (2018). Rajneeshpuram Was More than a Utopia in the Desert. It was a Mirror of the Time. *Humanities: The Magazine of the National Endowment for the Humanities* 39(2). www.neh.gov/humanities/2018/

spring/feature/rajneeshpuram-was-more-utopia-desert-it-was-mirror (accessed March 21, 2024).

Van Zandt, D. E. (1991). *Living in the Children of God*. Princeton: Princeton University Press.

Wadler, J. (1982). Moon's Marriage of the Masses. *The Washington Post*, July 2. www.washingtonpost.com/archive/lifestyle/1982/07/02/moons-marriage-of-the-masses/836806ee-b6d8-42d6-8e26-520456c19a7c/ (accessed October 31, 2022).

Walsh, R. (2008). Costume is Control in Polygamy. *The Salt Lake Tribune*, April 13. archive.sltrib.com/article.php?id=8908641&itype=NGPSID (accessed March 18, 2024).

Warner, C. (1979). "Archangel" Awaits Visitors from Space. *The Minneapolis Star*, March 15, p. 15B.

Watts, J. (1992). *God, Harlem U.S.A.: The Father Divine Story*. Berkeley: University of California Press.

Weisenfeld, J. (2016). *New World A-Coming: Black Religion and Racial Identity during the Great Migration*. New York: New York University Press.

Westbrook, D. A. (2022). *L. Ron Hubbard and Scientology Studies*. New York: Cambridge University Press.

Wheeler, K. R. (2021). Clothes of Righteousness: The MGT Uniform in the Twentieth Century. In A. Bigelow, ed., *Islam Through Objects*. London: Bloomsbury, pp. 26–38.

Wheeler, K. R. (2023). "Queens of the Earth": The MGT Uniform as a Form of Identity Creation and Nation Building. In M. W. Dallam & B. Zeller, eds., *Religion, Attire, and Adornment in North America*. New York: Columbia University Press, pp. 190–204.

Wild Wild Country. (2018). Directed by Maclain Way and Chapman Way [Documentary Series]. Netflix, episodes 1–6.

Wilson, B. R. (1975). *The Noble Savage: The Primitive Origins of Charisma*. Berkeley: University of California Press.

Wilson, E. (2008). Texas Ranch Moves from Raid toward Runway. *NYTimes.com*, July 3. www.nytimes.com/2008/07/03/us/03dress.html (accessed March 18, 2024).

Windsor Star (Windsor, Ontario, Canada). (1937). Nation-Wide Search Begun for Father Divine Aide, April 3, p. 10.

Wolfson, S. (2018). New York's Hot New Trend? Prairie Dresses Inspired by Orthodox Judaism. *TheGuardian.com*, September 14. www.theguardian.com/fashion/2018/sep/14/batsheva-hay-prairie-dresses-new-york-fashion-week (accessed March 18, 2024).

References

Woodard, J. B. & Mastin, T. (2005). Black Womanhood: "Essence" and its Treatment of Stereotypical Images of Black Women. *Journal of Black Studies* 36 (2), pp. 264–81.

The World (Coos Bay, Oregon). (1983). Candidate Terms Rajneesh Followers "Red-Clad Kooks," October 15, p. 2.

Wuthnow, R. (1998). *After Heaven: Spirituality in American Since the 1950s*. Berkeley: University of California Press.

X, A. (1967). Woman Praises Blessings She Found through Islam. *Muhammad Speaks*, April 21, p. 25.

X, F. (1967). Denver Sister Outlines Life of Muslims. *Muhammad Speaks*, January 13, p. 25.

X, M. J. (1967). Dignity of Muslims Seen at Savior's Day Meeting. *Muhammad Speaks*, March 17, p. 25.

X, S. D. (1967). Islam Can Save Black Man from the Fate of the Devil. *Muhammad Speaks*, April 14, p. 25.

Yam, K. (2018). Kate Hudson Dragged for 'Wild Wild Country'-Themed Halloween Costume. *Huffpost.com*, October 31. www.huffpost.com/entry/kate-hudson-wild-wild-country-halloween-costume_n_5bd9fadfe4b0da7bfc169d0f (accessed March 25, 2024).

Zeller, B. (2023). The Hare Krishna Look. In M. W. Dallam & B. E. Zeller, eds., *Religion, Attire, and Adornment in North America*. New York: Columbia University Press, pp. 295–319.

Cambridge Elements

New Religious Movements

Founding Editor
†James R. Lewis
Wuhan University

The late James R. Lewis was a Professor of Philosophy at Wuhan University, China. He was the author or co-author of 128 articles and reference book entries, and editor or co-editor of 50 books. He was also the general editor for the *Alternative Spirituality and Religion Review* and served as the associate editor for the *Journal of Religion and Violence*. His prolific publications include *The Cambridge Companion to Religion and Terrorism* (Cambridge University Press 2017) and *Falun Gong: Spiritual Warfare and Martyrdom* (Cambridge University Press 2018).

Series Editor
Rebecca Moore
San Diego State University

Rebecca Moore is Emerita Professor of Religious Studies at San Diego State University. She has written and edited numerous books and articles on Peoples Temple and the Jonestown tragedy. Publications include *Beyond Brainwashing: Perspectives on Cultic Violence* (Cambridge University Press 2018) and *Peoples Temple and Jonestown in the Twenty-First Century* (Cambridge University Press 2022). She is reviews editor for *Nova Religio*, the quarterly journal on new and emergent religions published by the University of Pennsylvania Press.

About the Series

Elements in New Religious Movements go beyond cult stereotypes and popular prejudices to present new religions and their adherents in a scholarly and engaging manner. Case studies of individual groups, such as Transcendental Meditation and Scientology, provide in-depth consideration of some of the most well known, and controversial, groups. Thematic examinations of women, children, science, technology, and other topics focus on specific issues unique to these groups. Historical analyses locate new religions in specific religious, social, political, and cultural contexts. These examinations demonstrate why some groups exist in tension with the wider society and why others live peaceably in the mainstream. The series highlights the differences, as well as the similarities, within this great variety of religious expressions. To discuss contributing to this series please contact Professor Moore.

Cambridge Elements

New Religious Movements

Elements in the Series

New Religious Movements and Comparative Religion
Olav Hammer and Karen Swartz

The New Witches of the West: Tradition, Liberation, and Power
Ethan Doyle White

The New Age Movement
Margrethe Løøv

Black Hebrew Israelites
Michael T. Miller

Anticultism in France: Scientology, Religious Freedom, and the Future of New and Minority Religions
Donald A. Westbrook

The Production of Entheogenic Communities in the United States
Brad Stoddard

Managing Religion and Religious Changes in Iran: A Socio-Legal Analysis
Sajjad Adeliyan Tous and James T. Richardson

Children in New Religious Movements
Sanja Nilsson

The Sacred Force of Star Wars Jedi
William Sims Bainbridge

Mormonism
Matthew Bowman

Jehovah's Witnesses
Jolene Chu and Ollimatti Peltonen

Wearing Their Faith: New Religious Movements, Dress, and Fashion in America
Lynn S. Neal

A full series listing is available at: www.cambridge.org/ENRM

www.ingramcontent.com/pod-product-compliance
Ingram Content Group UK Ltd.
Pitfield, Milton Keynes, MK11 3LW, UK
UKHW020006050225
454695UK00012B/79

9 781009 304658